A STORY ABOUT,
"I WILL NEVER DO NETWORK MARKETING"

JOE OCCHIOGROSSO

ISBN 978-0-9963652-0-8
Editor & Publisher: Melody Marler, Publishing Concierge, LLC
Cover Design: Dave Baker, Baker Group Utah

For information on quantity discounts or on having this title customized for your company, email joeobook@gmail.com.

Printed in the United States of America

Acknowledgments:
To my family, for all they have done for me over the years.
My parents Frank and Claire for their never-ending love and
support. My wife Annmarie who has been my rock through
all of my career choices and ventures and who puts up with my
hyper-social personality. Love you honey! Also a big thank you to
my brother John and my three amazing kids, Alex, Stephanie and
Frankie. And thanks to my business partner Frank Marone and
all the tens of thousands on my network marketing team.
I am nothing without you.

Praise for

A Story About, "I Will Never Do Network Marketing"

"Joe Occhiogrosso is the perfect person to have written this book because he actually *was* the prospect who said, 'I will never do network marketing.' I know this for a fact because I was the guy he said it to! Now, just a few years later, Joe has made millions of dollars in network marketing and, more importantly, he has helped thousands of people change their life through this amazing profession, including me and my family. Joe and I continue to build a tremendous business together to this day, and the guy who told me he'd 'NEVER do network marketing' has had me in his organization for over five years and counting."

– Bob Quintana, Network Marketing Millionaire, Author, Speaker, Trainer

"I worked with Joe on Wall Street back in the early 1990s and was also a network marketing skeptic for many years. It wasn't until just a few years ago that I decided to actually take the plunge and become a true professional in this amazing industry. Teaming up with Joe, I too quickly became a seven-figure annual earner. This book will help us all teach the masses that network marketing is simply a better way of living."

– Frank Marone, Seven-figure Earner Since 2011

"Until I was blessed to meet Joe O., I had no real understanding of what true leadership was all about. And this was after my 30-plus years as a successful corporate player and entrepreneur with an Ivy League and top B school education. Joe comes from a place of pure contribution. He paints a tapestry of life that makes us all want to be better. A model of inspiration, courage, and 'walking the talk,' Joe opens our eyes, hearts, and minds to perceive the world as a prism of potential and teaches us how to execute on that. In this 'must read' book, Joe tells it like it is—real-life illustrations of the challenges and rewards of the amazing network marketing business model, and how seasoned professionals ignite a kind of inner strength and fearless heart previously untapped in the more traditional world. The world is a better place with Joe Occhiogrosso. Anyone fortunate enough to be in his orbit becomes a bigger and better contributor and leader. I am eternally grateful for his leadership in the business of the 21st century."

– Susan Mazonson, Brown Alumni Association,
Board Member of the Association of Class Leaders,
MBA, University of Chicago, Booth School of Business

"Joe O. knows how to tell a great story—fill it with realistic characters and let them live their lives on the book's pages. Anyone who reads this book is certain to recognize similar characters, and similar situations from their own lives. And anyone who has ever made the decision to change their lives by building a personal business will see themselves in this story. Put yourself into this story, and choose your character. Will you be someone who gives up their dreams and slides back into the average lifestyle that holds so many people captive, or will you be one of the characters who tells YOUR story from stage, and inspires thousands of others to look beyond the everyday challenges? By telling this story, Joe is telling our stories. We just need to read it and make a decision."

– Bill Quain, Bestselling Author of over 20 Business Books

"For more than 20 years I've watched Joe empower professionals to business success. His dedication to helping others succeed is truly inspiring."

— Bart Oates, Esq., Three-time Super Bowl Champion and Entrepreneur

"This book really hit home for me because after I left Wall Street I was introduced to network marketing for the first time. As a single dad with four young children, I wanted to be there for my kids. Joe had quickly become one of my many mentors in this industry. With Joe's leadership and inspiration, I've come to believe what many are starting to realize: That life is way too short and that becoming a full-time network marketing professional can become a reality."

— Doug Borden, Former Equities Trader, Rumson, New Jersey

"As a career-long state trooper, I have always been skeptical about 'recruiting scam' businesses. However, something just made more sense the last time someone approached me. No one ever gets wealthy on a law enforcement salary, so over my 25-year career I've always had a second and third source of income. This time I'm happy to be building a sustainable residual income, which is creating a second pension for me. Thanks Joe O. for your leadership."

— Lieutenant Tony DiPaula, New Jersey State Police, Retired

"Network marketing was completely foreign to me just a few years ago. Then I was shown a video from a very well-respected local attorney and I soon realized that this was something very real. For years I was always one of the top producing real estate brokers in my county. I consistently made a great income but if I stopped working, the income stopped rolling in. Joe O. was instrumental in helping me lead my team and allowing me and so many others to create a significant life-changing residual income. In less than 18 months, with Joe's leadership and inspiration I have become a true network marketing professional and have been paying it forward to thousands on my team."

— Anthony Serino, Poughkeepsie, New York,
Real Estate Broker (retired), Mid-six-figure earner

"As a New York Police Chief, I have always been very skeptical of these 'pyramid-type' businesses. When my wife RaeAnn got involved a few years back, I was at first totally against it. Not until later, when I attended a meeting Joe O. spoke at, did I really 'get it.' Something clicked for me and my wife that night, and we are so happy it did. I soon retired from the police force and after just two years, I now make far more from my network marketing residuals than my 30-plus year pension provides us. Thanks Joe O.!"

— Brian Nichols, Police Chief, East Fishkill, New York (retired),
Network Marketing Professional, Six-figure-plus Earner

"I have never done anything like network marketing before. I started my career 30 years ago as a union pipefitter and then was so proud the day my wife and I finally ventured out to start what has become a very successful 'traditional' business. We invested our life savings into trucks and equipment and spent many stressful days and nights trying to manage the crew, quote estimates, and make a decent living. We've always done well but there was no end in sight. We didn't own a business—the business owned us. When an attorney friend of mine showed me this network marketing model, and the time freedom that it could provide, I was more than a little skeptical, but I eventually dove in 100%. I went from a complete novice just a few years ago to speaking in front of many thousands today, just telling my story of persistence. Joe O. is one of the best network marketing mentors you'll ever find. He's changed my life and the lives of many, and now I'm doing the same for others.

"Big" John & Lella Pyonteck, Network Marketing Professionals, Monroe
Township, New Jersey, Mid-six-figure Earners

"Joe O. has cracked the code for the small business owner and entrepreneur. The stories and lessons taught in this book shed a bright light on what it takes to succeed in today's modern world."

— Scott Fletcher, National Director, Primerica Financial Services

"Joe O. easily brings out the best in others, leads by example, and is an excellent mentor. His story is a real inspiration for anyone looking to learn how to take advantage of personal and financial opportunity."

— Michael Fallquist, CEO, Crius Energy

Contents

Foreword

Here is a book for "the rest of us": The millions of ordinary men and women who are regular, hard-working people. We pay our bills, take care of our families, go to church, send our children to the best schools we can, and dream of a better life. We don't want advice from celebrities, nor do we relate to stories about people who were in prison or on drugs before making it big. We have been looking for a book with a real-life story, and this book is just what we needed.

Joe O. wasn't a homeless person who pulled himself out of the gutter to create a fortune. Nor is he the son of rich parents who set him up in business—his dad was a police officer and his mom worked as a legal secretary. He is one of us—an ordinary person. Yet he reached deep into his imagination for a way to share his story of success.

If you are serious about making significant changes in your life, changes that will bring you wealth, stress-free living, and meaningful relationships with other successful people, then this is the book you have been waiting for.

The characters in this book were created to help convey the lessons that Joe O. actually learned and then used in building a million-dollar network marketing business in a very short time.

One of my favorite stories is the one about Joe's cousin Vito, who came to this country as a young immigrant and left many years later as a self-made millionaire. But even then he didn't stop. As a wealthy man back in his native Italy, Vito again set to work building a village. While the other characters in this story are fictional, Vito is a real person who created his own opportunity and left a legacy of hard work and success.

With straightforward language and great stories, Joe takes us on his journey of success. Thanks, Joe, for sharing this story. "The rest of us" appreciate it.

Bill Quain, Ph.D.
Bestselling author

Introduction

Most people are more afraid of success than they are of failure. Deep down, we all know our potential is limitless and this makes many people uncomfortable. Many people stop when they feel they are growing too much or too fast, and fear that they may become something too special. And that's a real shame. We were all put here to become as special as possible.

For many years I held myself back from my full potential by believing that my history as a highly trained Wall Street trader defined me as a certain kind of person, one who would not look at a business opportunity like network marketing. Somehow, I had the twisted notion that I would be wasting my education if I began a network marketing business.

What a mistake! When I finally let go of that notion, I embraced this profession and have never looked back.

Unfortunately, a lot of network marketing professionals don't approach those who are already successful in another profession, such as attorneys, bankers, investors, etc. But I have become fond of saying, *recruit up*! People who are already successful in another profession are those who will most likely immediately see the potential in network marketing.

The stories I tell in these pages through Big Eye, Cory, and their friends are many of those that I've told from stage, and to a lesser extent in my previous book, *The Power of Personal Equity*. My cousin Vito is real, and that's his real name and his story. All of the other characters in the book are fictional, designed to help share the lessons I've found so useful in building a multi-million dollar network marketing business.

I hope you will enjoy this story, and I would be honored if you would take the time to write a brief review on Amazon. Also, please feel free to reach out to me by email, at joeobook@gmail.com.

I wrote this book to reassure you that you can have it all. You deserve it all. Anything less is being disrespectful to your Maker.

– *Joe Occhiogrosso*

CHAPTER 1

The Best Day of the Week

Sunday. It was Cory's favorite day of the week. The entire family was home. The house was cozy and a little chaotic, and the aroma of dinner in the oven drifted through the room. Sunday was the day that truly meant family to Cory.

He and Michelle were lucky to have this, Cory realized— young teenage kids who liked to hang out with their parents. It was bitterly cold outside, but this room was warm and full of love. He closed his eyes and took it all in. Even the noise from the television in the background appealed to him right now.

Cory couldn't help but overhear his son's animated conversation as Michael told his grandmother about this morning's hockey game. "And Gram, I scored the winning goal! It was a power play and I just happened to be in the right spot—it was a great pass, and I flicked it right into the net!"

Cory smiled as he listened to his son. Michael was a young teenager, usually so reserved and a little self-conscious. But today, he was glowing as he recounted the game highlights to his grandmother.

Cory remembered his own days as a high school varsity athlete. The winning goal! The winning run! Once you experienced that high, nothing really came close to it.

After getting into his job as a trader on Wall Street, that high for Cory became making a great trade on the floor. Making a great deal, entertaining, connecting people—that had become his life.

He frowned as thoughts of work intruded on his perfect afternoon. At one time, his accomplishments at work had been his proudest achievements. Graduating from an Ivy League school with his MBA—how proud he and his parents were the day he received that diploma. And his wife's parents were impressed!

But that was years ago. Looking over at his children, Cory had the stark realization of how precious this Sunday was with them—how precious every day with them was. And how now, his greatest high was right here, in this room, with his family.

The familiar introduction to the television program beginning in the next room startled Cory out of his reflection.

Tick, tick, tick, tick, tick.

*Oh **no!*** he thought. ***60 Minutes** is on! My weekend is over and I have to go to work tomorrow.*

As the introduction to *60 Minutes* came on, Cory realized this sweet weekend was almost over; impending dread settled in his chest as his thoughts turned to the week ahead. It was sure to be busy. He hadn't even looked at that report that was due Monday, since ditching his briefcase in the den on Friday after work.

"Dad!" Michael was calling from the other side of the room. "Dad? Are you listening?"

Cory looked up and realized he'd slumped into his chair, thinking about his busy workweek.

"You'll be at my game tomorrow night, right? Gram's coming!"

Cory assured Michael he would be there, and got up to turn down the sound on the TV. This used to be his favorite program, and now it made him gloomy just to hear the sound of the ticking clock.

After dinner, Cory and Michelle chatted as they cleaned up the dishes. Cory reluctantly excused himself to get organized for the crazy week that surely awaited him. This used to be the best part of his week, Cory remembered. He used to sit alone in the den, writing out his schedule and appointments for the week, thinking about which days he'd be available to get out on the town and entertain clients.

Cory also used to get to the gym every night after work. But now, he just wanted to get home as early as possible. What if Michael had a game? Or if his daughter Elizabeth wanted to go to the gym to work out for the upcoming soccer season? She had started looking at colleges, and had mentioned some applications she needed to send in soon.

Sighing, Cory scribbled some notes about his new client in the margins of the agenda for the Monday morning meeting. When had he started dreading meeting new clients? Late nights entertaining clients and friends, and still arriving at work bright and fresh the next day, had once been his signature. At one time, it was all he'd needed, and he had thought it was his dream life.

But that was 20 years ago, and things had changed.

CHAPTER 2

Disaster

Cory gripped the steering wheel as traffic crawled along the expressway. Expressway—what a joke! It was no expressway today. An unexpected winter blizzard had crippled the city a couple of days ago, and subzero temperatures had quickly settled in as soon as the storm had cleared. It appeared the deep freeze would last a few days.

To top it off, work at the bank had been crazy today. The directors were making up for the snow day they'd all been forced to take when the city shut down during the blizzard.

Cory impatiently flipped through a few radio stations as he waited for traffic to move, crawling along through the bitter cold, finally snapping the music off. There was no way he would make it to Michael's hockey game tonight. "It's probably third period by now," Cory mumbled to himself.

Reaching his exit at last, he wound through the suburban streets, pulled into his garage and switched off the engine. The house was completely dark, the same as when he'd left it. Now he remembered—Michelle had left work early to pick the kids up from school and take them to eat with Gram before the hockey game. No one had been home since this morning.

Juggling his briefcase and slipping off his coat, he opened the door into the small mudroom in the breezeway, and then slid open the pocket door to the laundry room.

He drew a breath of frigid air. Man, the house was cold! And what was that sound? Had someone left the faucet on? He could hear water running, and it wasn't just trickling. Irritated, Cory flipped on the light in the laundry room. The faucet wasn't on, but the floor was submerged in water.

"What the hell?" he blurted. He flung open the cabinet underneath the utility sink and sure enough, water was pouring out of a pipe. It must have frozen and burst during the day while everyone was at work and school. Cory swore again, and ran to the shutoff valve to stop the flow.

Frantically paging through the contacts on his phone, he found the number for the plumber, Dave, who had helped them a few years ago. *That guy can do anything, and he's always so calm under pressure,* Cory thought. *I hope he isn't busy with a bunch of people like me calling him tonight.*

The adjoining kitchen and family rooms were also flooded, and Cory stepped up onto the stairway as he dialed. After three rings, Cory started to panic. He started to think about who else did plumbing, when finally, Dave answered.

"Hey, Dave, I'm sorry to be calling so late," Cory said. "This is Cory Anderson. You helped us with plumbing on our addition a few years ago and I've come home to a flood! The furnace seems to be out, and we had some pipes burst. Any chance you could help us? I've turned off the water but..." Cory trailed off as he looked back at the flooded rooms.

Dave whistled. "Wow, major bummer, man! It must be really cold there," he said. "I'm in Arizona, so it's not really that late here, so no worries! I'm just finishing a round of golf. And I don't work in plumbing anymore. Sold the business. I'm actually semi-retired. But I can refer you to someone. Hang on a second."

While he waited for the number, Cory tried to remember what he could about Dave. He was too young to retire—he must have a family vacation home in Arizona.

As Dave came back on the line, Cory could hear laughter in the background. Dave gave Cory the number for the young guy who had purchased the plumbing business.

Cory couldn't resist. "So, Dave, how did you manage to retire? As I remember, you're my age! What happened?"

Dave laughed. "I'm only semi-retired Cory," he said. "I started a new business that's gone really well and it's on cruise control now. So I sold the plumbing business. I don't have to worry about managing three different crews, my trucks breaking down, employees calling in sick, or about business insurance. And, I live in Arizona now during the winter. I'm making more in a *month* than I used to make in some bad *years!*"

"I'd give a lot to be living in Arizona right now," Cory said, eyeing the water. He rubbed his temples with the palms of his hand. "I'd better find the wet-dry vac right now, but I'd like to hear more about this business when you get back in the spring."

"I'm actually coming home this weekend for a family wedding," Dave said. "I'll call you for coffee."

They agreed on a time, and Cory called the new plumber. He got to work vacuuming up the water while he waited for the new plumber to arrive.

What would it be like to spend winters in Arizona? Cory thought. *No icy commute through horrendous traffic, no burst pipes, no blizzards shutting down the expressway.*

Semi-retired? Really?

CHAPTER 3

Disaster Meets Opportunity

True to his word, Dave invited Cory for Sunday morning coffee. He showed up at the coffee shop with a laptop.

They ordered coffee and took a table near the window.

"So, you sell computers now? Or software?" Cory cracked.

Dave laughed. "No, I've never been much of a tech guy, but I have a short video that will tell you about my company better than I can. Then when we're done I'm going to call a colleague who can answer any questions you may have. He's been doing this business longer than I have. In fact, he used to be a big shot on Wall Street like you!"

"A video? Man, you must have a huge marketing budget!" Cory said.

Dave just smiled, logged onto the Wi-Fi, and sipped his coffee while he waited for the website to load. As the video played, Cory became more and more intrigued. He had heard of this business model—network marketing. He didn't personally know anyone involved in it. Well, now he did—he knew Dave.

But his friends and colleagues occasionally made jokes about people in these businesses—they called these companies "get-rich-quick" and "pyramid" schemes. He'd heard of people who had alienated their family members and friends, convinced that they could become a millionaire in a month if only everyone would join them! Now that he thought about it, he remembered his uncle had tried network marketing once, and the results were disastrous. Now that he was adding his colleagues and family into the equation, Cory started to get a little queasy.

Dave sensed Cory's discomfort and after the video was done, picked up his phone. "Hang on a second, Cory. I know you'll have questions. We're going to call Big Eye. He's one of my mentors in this company, and he can answer any questions you have."

Big Eye answered on the second ring, and greeted Dave warmly. Dave put the phone on speaker.

"Big Eye, I'm sitting here with Cory Anderson, a former plumbing client from town who happens to work on Wall Street like you used to a few years ago. Cory, this is Big Eye. He's one of my mentors and business partners. He's been doing this quite a bit longer than me and always makes himself available to answer any questions new people like you may have."

"Hi, Big Guy is it?" Cory said.

"Close enough," Big Eye said. "So what do you do on the Street?"

"I trade institutional bonds and currencies," Cory said. "Well, I used to, but now I'm also in management, which has really been a drag for the last few years."

"I can relate. I was in that fast–paced world for over 10 years—all through my twenties and early thirties," Big Eye said quickly. "I was making great money and had some good times, but I knew there had to be a better way to make a great income without all the stress and time poverty. So what questions do you have for me?"

Cory hesitated for a few seconds.

Time poverty. He had never heard that term before. He regained his thoughts and said, "I see how it works. But I don't know if this is for me. I'm not wired to work that way and neither is my network, honestly," Cory said.

"That's what I thought too, at first," Big Eye admitted. "However, when I saw the lifestyle that some of the leaders were enjoying, I had to take a serious look. That's when I got hooked on residual income and working from home. Cory, I can tell from your questions this business might interest you. I'll be in the city tomorrow for an opportunity meeting, but I'll have a little bit of time right before, if you want to meet for a quick drink after work," Big Eye said. "But it will have to be quick. I believe there are about 500 people registered, so I need to get there early."

Cory agreed, and Big Eye ended the call quickly.

Cory turned to Dave. "Join us?" he asked.

"Sorry," Dave said. "My flight back to Arizona is at 6 a.m., and I have a tee time tomorrow afternoon. But go, meet Big Eye! He will answer every concern you have. And besides, you're two peas in a pod." He winked at Cory, and packed up his laptop.

Tee time? It was the middle of January.

CHAPTER 4

Why Are You Here?

Cory walked into the hotel lounge and looked around the room as he stomped snow off his boots. He immediately spotted a smartly dressed man in jeans, a sharp shirt, and a sport jacket, sitting at the edge of the bar right next to the door. The man looked very relaxed, and with a warm smile raised his hand to greet Cory.

"Big Eye?" Cory asked.

"Pleased to meet you Cory," Big Eye replied, standing up to shake Cory's hand. *He's not an especially tall or big man,* Cory thought. *I wonder where he got that nickname?*

They placed their drink orders, and settled into bar stools.

"So Cory, have you thought of more questions for me about creating your dream life? What are your concerns about this business?" Big Eye asked.

Cory had been working hard on Wall Street for almost 20 years now. He thought he *had* been building his dream life. He'd made a solid six figures, complete with big yearly bonuses, for almost two decades now. They had been able to buy a nice five-bedroom home in the suburbs and one down the shore, but both homes had big mortgages and sky-high property taxes. The family took nice vacations and their kids, Michael and Elizabeth, were exceptional athletes and students. But all told, Cory estimated he only brought home 51% of his pay, given his tax bracket. Most of his family and friends assumed he must be "financially secure" or rich, but in reality, his family would be in deep trouble if he were to be suddenly downsized tomorrow.

Cory laughed. "Well, is it possible? A dream life, I mean? I've been working my tail off for years and my wife and I have only managed to save enough to send one of my two kids to college—and that's a state school! Who knows where they will actually want to go."

"Oh, it's more than possible Cory," Big Eye said.

"Well, then I'm all ears," Cory answered. "One thing that does worry me though, honestly. I'm concerned that people will think I'm a failure at my 'real' job, that I've lost my mind, or maybe that I've been brainwashed. My uncle had a really bad experience with network marketing. And it seems like a lot of people go from living in their cars to becoming overnight millionaires. I just don't see how it's possible."

Big Eye took a sip of his sparkling mineral water and swiveled to face Cory. "I have a few suggestions for addressing those thoughts, but first you mentioned worrying about people thinking you're a failure at your 'real' job. Do you feel successful now? What is success to you? Money, cars, vacations? It sounds like you already have those things. So—why are you here?"

He was caught off guard by Big Eye's direct line of questioning. *Wow, this guy really cuts to the chase,* Cory thought.

Aloud, he answered, "Well, my day starts at 5 a.m. and I

sometimes don't get home until after 7:30 or even later. I have to travel overseas a lot to see clients in London. I used to enjoy it, but since my children are getting older and have more activities, I don't want to keep missing out on everything. And the firm is always bringing in new graduates who they could easily train to do my job for half of what I get paid. That's on my mind every single day. It's happened to a few colleagues. If I got downsized …"

Cory looked up. "I never really considered working from home. I mean, I spent years and tens of thousands of dollars on my MBA. But Dave spent years and years getting his plumbing business established, and worked really long hours to keep it that way. And now he says he is semi-retired. He doesn't have to deal with commuting or trucks or liability insurance. I want that life. I am not afraid to work hard, but I never really thought I could make a successful Wall Street-level living from my house."

> First of all, no one is telling you to quit your job to do this business.

"First of all, no one is telling you to quit your job to do this business, Cory," Big Eye said. "But you're right, and you see Dave succeeding and his income skyrocketing, while he works part-time and plays golf. Do you think he's more talented or smarter than you? Even if he was, you can still do it. It's a matter of conviction. What do you want for you and your family? And, if you're worried about what people will think about you—that can actually be a good thing. This business is about coming out of your comfort zone. I have personally watched 'Dave the Plumber' go from a guy who just three years ago would hesitate to say even a few words in front of a small room, to being one of our company's most dynamic and talented storytellers. At our last convention he spoke in front of more than 10,000 people. He killed it and we couldn't get him off the stage. We tease him about it all the time."

They both laughed at this—Cory, at the idea of it, and Big Eye, at the memory.

Big Eye continued, "The most expensive thing we own is time. If you want more time with your family we can dig in deeper, and I can tell you my story, where I came from, and how I got to the point where I stopped worrying about what other people thought almost immediately. Even though some people may think otherwise, your diploma does not define you. This business can really open up your mind."

"I just can't get past what my uncle said about his experience in network marketing," Cory admitted. "He said he got stuck with a garage full of stuff and a bunch of greedy people at the top who disappeared after he bought it all. He thought it was a scam."

"I have to go in a minute, so let me put this conversation into a different perspective, give you something to think about," Big Eye countered. "Would some people say Wall Street is a scam?"

Surprised, Cory put down his glass. "Well, yeah, lots of people hate Wall Street. They think it's a bunch of greedy people making lots of money. But I'm not greedy. I work hard and I'm honest."

"So you're telling me Wall Street is not a scam? That it's not true, what some people say? That everyone is not greedy, that there are a lot of good smart hardworking intelligent people?"

"Of course!" Cory said.

"Well, don't you think that might be the same thing for network marketing?" Big Eye asked. "That there are good and bad people, and negative connotations that aren't justified, just like any industry?"

"I guess you're right," Cory said. "All I ever wanted was to get my MBA and end up as a trader on Wall Street. Mission accomplished! I used to love my job, but now that I'm in management, I'm mostly just miserable. That's what actually piqued my interest in what Dave was doing."

"Well, that sounds familiar too!" Big Eye said. "Aren't some of your colleagues happy, though?"

"Oh, yeah, most of them are," Cory agreed quickly. "But they're in my old department—not the new one I took on."

Big Eye nodded. "Been there too," he said. "Let me ask you something. When Dave first mentioned that our business was network marketing, what was your first thought?"

"Well I told him the business was intriguing—really interesting to me. I also told him we have to hear about my uncle's bad experience at every family reunion. And, my network isn't wired to accept the network marketing business model. In fact, one guy calls it multilevel marketing," Cory said.

> It is multilevel marketing. What would you prefer, single-level marketing? There's no leverage in that.

"It *is* multilevel marketing," Big Eye said, laughing. "What would you prefer, single-level marketing? There's no leverage in that."

Big Eye finished his drink and stood up. "And right now, I've got to go teach some hungry new people how to achieve their goals!" he said. "You're welcome to come to one of these opportunity meetings sometime, if you'd like. There are always a lot of curious people there, so you would fit right in. Just let me know and I'll make sure I save you a seat. Most of my engagements fill up with standing room only. "

Big Eye picked up his jacket from the back of the bar stool and folded it over his arm. "That actually sounded kind of arrogant, Cory, and I didn't mean it that way. It's just that I don't speak at these meetings all the time. Only about once every few weeks. Since I'm one of the top income-earners in our company, people want to hear how it's done. And they like my stories! That's all." Big Eye smiled and Cory stood to shake his hand.

Cory thanked Big Eye for his time and slipped his coat back on. As Big Eye walked toward the exit, a few people stood from a nearby table and greeted him. A few asked him to pose for a photo with him. *Photos?* Cory thought.

By the time Big Eye reached the mezzanine, he had collected quite an entourage of happy fans. Cory waited a few minutes and then approached one of the guys who had asked Big Eye for a photo. Innocently, Cory asked, "Who was that guy and why did you want a photo with him?" The man answered, "He's just a friend—one who just happened to save my house and my marriage last year."

Cory had a lot on his mind as he headed home. *Wall Street, a scam?* he thought. *What a shocking statement. And yet, those who don't make it on Wall Street may actually think that.*

CHAPTER 5

Network Marketing is Weatherproof

Another northeaster had swept through overnight, burying the city and suburbs in yet another blanket of heavy, drifting snow. Waking up to weather closures and travel warnings, Big Eye just smiled. He had a second cup of coffee before dressing in his gym clothes and heading out the door.

Big Eye reached the gym just as the snowplow finished clearing the lot. He waved to the driver, and jogged into the gym.

"Good morning!" the desk clerk said. "Not too many hardy souls out this early after the storm!"

"This is the highlight of my day," said Big Eye, swiping his membership card over the reader. On his way upstairs to his favorite elliptical machine, Big Eye greeted several neighbors, who were also apparently taking advantage of the snow day to get in an early workout. Big Eye adjusted his headphones and switched over to his audiobook collection. He was in the mood for some inspiration this morning—maybe one of the classics from Jim Rohn or Anthony Robbins.

About halfway through his workout, Big Eye felt a tap on his shoulder. He looked up to see Cory.

"Hey!" Big Eye said. "Haven't seen you here before."

"I was hoping that was you!" Cory said. "Thought I'd take a chance. I have a snow day, so I don't have to commute to the office. I usually go to the gym in the city." Cory's cell phone started buzzing in his pocket, and he glanced down and sighed. "But apparently my clients in Europe don't care if we are snowed in."

"The market never sleeps!" Big Eye chimed in.

"I don't mean to interrupt," Cory said.

"Not a problem," Big Eye said, looping his earbuds over his shoulders and gesturing to the machine next to him.

"It's just that you mentioned you had more stories. We didn't have much time, when we met before your event, although I really appreciated you taking the time," Cory added quickly. "But I'd really like to hear more of your story. It seems like we have similar backgrounds."

"Sure!" Big Eye said. "This morning I was actually just thinking again about my experience with dipping my toe into network marketing. It was the storm that brought it to mind. When you think about it, network marketing is weatherproof. When you live in the northeast, like we do, and you occasionally get snowed in, the advantages of a home-based business multiply."

"I can certainly see that," Cory said. "Our bank is closed today. State of emergency in the city, so no one will be able to go into work today. But you know what that means for tomorrow! Double-time." His phone buzzed again.

"That's so true," Big Eye said, nodding toward Cory's phone as Cory looked down at the number.

Ignoring the call, Cory started punching buttons on his

elliptical and started slowly warming up. These machines were quiet, so they could actually talk and work out at the same time.

"I'm really interested in how you got started, especially coming from Wall Street," Cory said.

"Ah yes," Big Eye said. This was a little unusual, out of his workout routine, but hey—it was a snow day, so he might as well take his time. Besides, Cory was smart and eager, and reminded Big Eye of himself five or six years ago.

Big Eye slowed his pace to accommodate Cory's warm up gait.

"When someone first mentioned the concept of network marketing to me, I didn't really pay attention. I loved the idea of starting a part-time business career that would pay me residuals, but I didn't think it could possibly pay enough to make it worth my while," Big Eye started, while Cory warmed up. "If you're not familiar with the concept of residuals, it means I would continue to be paid on an initial sale every time one of my customers consumed the product and re-ordered. In addition, if I mentored others to become successful distributors, I received a percentage of their sales. This was a traditional network marketing company."

Cory nodded knowingly. "I understand residual income," he said. "Very appealing."

"Besides the residuals, I loved helping people come out of their shell and become bigger, better people. This business opportunity allowed me to grow in so many ways that my job never provided, but the best part is that I found a system that actually pays based on how many people I help," Big Eye said. "It's funny, at my old firm I was one of just a few dozen 'partners' who were supposed to lead the firm to new heights. On paper, and legally, we were actual partners. But the truth is, I really could only trust a handful of my fellow partners. Lots of my colleagues were alpha male dogs eating the weaker dogs. With network marketing, though, you can really only succeed by helping others."

Cory smiled again. "I am all too familiar with the dog-eat-dog world!" he said. "There are a lot of guys at my work who really love their jobs. I just don't happen to, at least not at the moment. But I did once."

"Well, I certainly understand that!" Big Eye said. "When I was first introduced to network marketing, I attended a few meetings about 20 years ago, signed up as a representative, and soon made a few sales. But it was definitely a part-time startup, and I was still a slave to my trading desk, my one-hour commute to the suburbs, and my career. This was in the days before cell phones, so there was no working commute. A commute was just that: One hour of driving each way. I told myself I didn't have the time or energy to build a solid side business," Big Eye said. "I didn't really launch into network marketing then, but I'm eternally grateful for that first experience. It planted a seed in my mind about residual income and the benefits of starting my own business—any business. I learned a lot about tax write-offs and other secrets of the wealth-builders and also gained a newfound respect for the network marketing profession. I finally understood the concept of leverage and helping others while helping myself. To me, it made a ton of sense."

"Why didn't you really take off with network marketing then?" Cory asked.

"Instead of really concentrating on the network marketing company, I actually chose to go into a traditional business," Big Eye said. "But I soon realized that among other things, on a day like today—a snow emergency day—you still have to pay employees, plow the lot, do what you can to run business as usual without any help. But if you rely on customers coming into your store, they couldn't on a day like this, because everyone's snowed in! Old-fashioned business is not all it's cracked up to be. Each year it gets harder."

"Right?" Cory said. "A lot of people are literally stuck in their homes today. I'm lucky—I live close enough to walk here."

"Not only is network marketing wonderful in that you can work from your home, it's also weatherproof. Bad weather or good weather—neither one slows your business down," Big Eye said. "On the day when you know most of your team will be homebound, you can take the time to have training sessions. You're certainly not too busy, and your prospects aren't too busy. So it's a great opportunity to be watching training videos or host a conference call. Even if you lose power, you can still use a cell phone. We live in an amazing time, with Wi-Fi everywhere, Skype, online conferencing, Face Time, free conference calls. There's virtually no reason you can't supplement or make a full-time income. No matter where you are or what it's like outside, you can always roll up your sleeves and expose your business to people who need to know about it."

"I'd really like to give this business a shot," Cory said. "I'm impressed with you, and Dave—well, he's semi-retired! But, can real people make real money?"

Before Big Eye could answer, Cory added, "And honestly, I'm still not sure what to say to people who shut me down when they hear it's network marketing."

"For over 20 years, I didn't believe this model of business could work—even though I knew a few people who made it work for them. I always had a deep respect for these people because I knew it wasn't easy," Big Eye answered. "Nothing worthwhile in life is easy, right? But making more money than ever before from the comfort of your own home? Lounging around in your workout clothes while others commute back and forth to work? Regardless of the weather? Any day of the week? Is it being done? Can it be done? Absolutely."

Big Eye spread his hands wide and slowed his pace. "I'm doing it right here, now! But for a long time, I completely disregarded these types of businesses. Not that I didn't think they were legit. I knew a few that were legendary mega-businesses, so unlike many others, I didn't prejudge, never had any close-minded ideas that they were all 'pyramid schemes.' But still, I was worried about what other people would say about me. I certainly understand that concern, Cory, and so do most people in this business."

"I've always been open-minded about business," Cory said. "And deep down, I've wondered if I'm an entrepreneur. I love the TV show where regular people come in and pitch their ideas to the wealthy businesspeople. But the question is always asked: 'How are you going to get your product to the market? How are you doing it now?' Honestly, network marketing seems like word-of-mouth recommendations to me."

"That's exactly what it is," Big Eye said. "It makes too much sense to ignore. I've always been open-minded about any business model that's been proven, and I was aware that this could work exceptionally well for people who knew what they were doing. I had tremendous respect for anyone who was successful at it. I have to admit, though, I was a little hesitant at first because of the stigma. It's often more socially acceptable to say I'm a Wall Street trader or a traditional local business owner than to tell people I'm involved in a direct-selling or network marketing business. But I wasn't bothered as much by the stigma or by using the model as a way to make a living as I was by the way I thought people might react to me. I now know these silly comfort zones of 'fitting in' come with a price, and sometimes a steep one. Now that I've become one of the most successful network marketers in the world and enjoy a lifestyle beyond most people's dreams, I don't care what people think or say. The lesson? I shouldn't have worried before either."

> I now know these silly comfort zones of "fitting in" come with a price—and sometimes a steep one.

Cory slowed his pace again, listening intently. These were exactly his concerns, but somehow Big Eye had burst through his self-doubts and now lived a most satisfying lifestyle.

"Here's a good analogy, Cory. Have you ever bought or sold a home?" Big Eye asked.

"Of course," Cory said. "I have two—one here, and one at the shore."

"OK. So you're familiar with Realtors then," Big Eye said.

"Of course!" Cory said again.

"Well think of it this way," Big Eye said. "A typical home-based business leverages the work of others and pays based on self-starter productivity, just like the model used by your local real estate brokers and agents. Did you buy your home from an undercover agent in a pyramid scheme? After all, the real estate broker holds the license and gets a cut of sales from all property sold by a network of multi-level agents. Some agents list the home and bring the buyer and get paid most of the 5 to 6 percent commission, but the broker always gets a share for setting up the operation. A real estate agent who hustles and makes a lot of connections can make more than a decent living listing and selling houses for clients. At the end of the year, they can surely make more than their broker. In addition, there's nothing stopping them from spinning off and becoming a broker or investor themselves. Some successful agents aspire to become a broker someday, and others enjoy just being an agent. They like their side of the system because they have fewer worries, minimal overhead, and a pure pay-for-performance business model."

"Never thought of Realtors in this way, but you're exactly right," Cory said.

"As you know, this model of real estate brokerage in which the broker leverages the time and efforts of his or her agents isn't completely home-based. Often the broker has a local office that the agents use as their base, but they don't make their money sitting in the office pushing paper. It's about networking, making connections," Big Eye continued.

"Right," Cory said. Big Eye paused as Cory contemplated this new perspective.

"I get the sense that a lot of your hesitation comes from the initial reaction you've gotten from your friends and family, particularly your uncle," Big Eye said.

Cory nodded.

"Most likely, your uncle never fully understood home-based businesses because he was introduced by someone who didn't understand, or didn't do a good job of teaching the business model," Big Eye said. "This happens a lot. People don't realize how much damage they can do by not understanding the right way to start a network marketing business. In my first network marketing company, I was lacking the conviction needed to succeed in a big way. I wasn't 'all-in.' Although I knew the guy drawing circles in front of the room was being honest about his residual income and the 'sky's the limit opportunity,' I just wasn't ready—mentally, physically, or spiritually. I do regret not being more focused and open-minded at the time. I may have been retired much sooner if I'd gotten serious about network marketing 15 years ago. But without the Internet, email, and cell phones, it would've taken a lot of time and effort to work a second business from home and keep it alive and prosperous, even if I had been ready. Today we live in a completely different world. With today's technology and gadgets, there's no reason we can't make millions from our smart phones. The network marketing profession is going to grow exponentially this coming decade."

Big Eye slowed his elliptical and checked his stats. "That's it for me," he said. "Time to go home and take a few three-way calls."

"I'm in," Cory said quickly. "I'm going to give this business a shot. I'm ready."

"Congratulations," Big Eye said. "Dave will be happy, too. Welcome to the team."

CHAPTER 6

The Shutdown

Cory really was ready. Almost immediately, he signed up several customers. Dave was his go-to guy for the three-way call, which Cory used every time he showed the video to a prospect. Even his friends and family were excited about the new business. Cory was becoming more confident with every presentation, but still hanging on to his Wall Street job. He was burning the candle at both ends, but he was happy and optimistic.

In preparation for an upcoming weekend retreat with his colleagues from Wall Street, Cory downloaded a new personal development audiobook for the trip, and hopped on the shuttle to the airport. This was going to be fun! He was looking forward to visiting with the guys from his old department.

Arriving upstate at the remote lodge, the team unpacked quickly and met for drinks in the gathering room. The massive fireplace cast a warm glow around the room and the wait staff circulated with hors d'oeuvres and a tray of drinks. Everyone chatted amiably, the frantic work left behind for the weekend.

"Hey Cory!" Cory turned to see Bill, one of his best friends from his old department.

"Hey! Good to see you here!" Cory said, genuinely pleased to see his old friend. He hadn't seen Bill on the quick shuttle flight up to the lodge, but they lived in neighboring suburbs and had always been friendly colleagues when they were in the same department. Since Cory had been promoted to management and moved to a different floor, they didn't run into each other much anymore.

"What's new, man?" Bill asked, snagging a drink from the passing waiter's tray with one hand, and nibbling on a cheese appetizer with the other.

"Same old stuff at work," Cory said. "Kids and Michelle are great! And I've started a new side business that I'm working from home. It's going really well so far, and my team is growing fast!"

Bill stopped chewing, and looked at Cory. "What is it?" he asked.

"I have a video I can show you. It explains way better than I ever could," Cory said, reaching for his phone.

Bill's eyes narrowed and he held up his hand. "I don't want to see a video," he said. "It's a pyramid scam, isn't it? They always rope you in with those crazy videos showing people on yachts and then bam, you have a garage full of shampoo. You'll lose your hair before you can go through all the crap you bought at inflated prices."

"It's not a scam!" Cory replied hastily.

But Bill's loud and hasty rebuke had attracted the attention of a couple of guys talking nearby and they quickly joined the conversation. "Cory's in a pyramid scam?" one of the men said. "Dude! I thought you were Ivy League."

"It's not a scam," Cory protested. "Here, if you could just watch this."

The three men laughed and waved him off. They wandered away, and as they joined another group, they made gestures back toward Cory, laughing. Cory's face burned with shame and he felt sick to his stomach. Fortunately, the retreat leader began the program, and Cory turned to focus on the speaker. This was going to be a long weekend.

On Monday morning, Cory was still feeling nauseous and mortified. He got to work early and closed himself in his office. He slogged through the endless day, but finally, Cory was in his car, headed home. At least there was an opportunity meeting tonight. And it was in his own town, with Big Eye as the speaker. It would be packed, and Cory couldn't wait. He needed the encouragement, and a little anonymity.

Big Eye was circulating through the room, greeting the people he knew and introducing himself to the ones he didn't. Cory was always amazed at this—the guy didn't have to be friendly to the beginners, or those on other teams. He just genuinely seemed to love what he did, and it was clear that helping other people had become his *why* in life.

"Whoa. Rough weekend?" Big Eye said as Cory walked over to greet him.

"You could say that," Cory said, shaking Big Eye's hand. "I got shut down pretty hard at our company retreat Friday night, and I've been feeling really physically sick ever since. I wasn't even trying to sign anyone up! I was just excited about telling the guys what I was doing now."

As he briefly retold the story, Cory's confusion and hurt feelings were clear. His resolve was clearly shaken.

When Cory finished, Big Eye said quietly, "I have a question for you Cory. How many of those guys do you think merely 'exist,' compared to those who enjoy their dream lives? Why do so few people get what they want out of life? The answer is they don't know how to create it. Unfortunately, a lot of them are cynical and put down other people who are trying to create a dream life."

Cory looked down, as the embarrassment he'd suffered at the retreat washed over him again.

"Think about it Cory," Big Eye said. "Those guys drive or take a train each way an hour into town. They leave home in the dark and come home in the dark. People who commute this way spend three to four months a year in the dark. It seems like half your life is spent in bumper-to-bumper traffic. What will they do when they get home? Put dinner on the table, help their kids do homework, maybe break out the laptop after the kids go to bed and work for a few more hours. And they make fun of you? These are the people who can't get over themselves. They know there are people who are not as smart, educated, or connected, who are making network marketing work for them. They just don't have the guts to go for it."

> These are the people who can't get over themselves. They know there are people who are not as smart, educated, connected, who are making network marketing work for them. They just don't have the guts to go for it.

Cory still didn't speak, but he was perking up a bit. Big Eye glanced toward the podium and saw that he would need to get to the stage. He placed a hand on Cory's shoulder.

"Look, when you tried to show your colleague what you were excited about, I'll bet you thought he would take a look—that he would at least be happy for you," Big Eye said.

"Yes!" Cory said. "That's exactly what I expected. I didn't expect to be the punching bag of the weekend."

"I need to get this meeting started now," Big Eye said. "But you've given me an idea and I'm going to change up my topic a little tonight. I have another story that might help you." Big Eye clapped Cory on the back and headed up to the podium to greet the meeting organizer. As Cory turned to find a seat, he noticed Dave, waving and gesturing to an empty seat.

"Hey, I didn't know you were in town," Cory said.

"Just for a day. I heard Big Eye was speaking," Dave said. "He's been speaking at events as long as I've been with the company. He was always good on stage, but every time I hear him, he just gets better. I don't know where he gets all these great stories. He seems to glean stories from almost every experience, and make them relevant and engaging."

Cory started to tell Dave about the retreat fiasco, but the roar of the crowd signaled Big Eye's arrival onstage. Without any preamble, Big Eye dove straight into his topic.

"Network marketing may well be the most misunderstood marketing channel of all time. People who have no clue how it works may dismiss it as a 'pyramid scheme,' which is pure ignorance. It also gets a bad rap because of the people have lost a few hundred bucks start-up money, and their self-esteem, failing at it. Most of these failures are due to a lack of training—failing to teach people a simple, proven way to build their businesses."

Big Eye paused and gestured to a man in the front row. "My business partner Frank likes to say, 'No one ever fails in a good network marketing business; they just quit before they reach their goals.' Solid MLM companies conduct serious business and should be taken seriously by anyone who wants serious results."

The audience murmured its assent.

"Let me tell you a story," Big Eye said, and the audience visibly settled. It was clear his audience loved Big Eye's stories.

Dave laughed and poked Cory. "A new story!" he said.

"Have you ever thought about how new and great ideas evolve, and come to be accepted? At first they're laughed at and called ridiculous. Then they're vehemently opposed, but eventually they're accepted as universal truth.

"Over the last 200 years, the Western world has gone from the farming era to the Industrial Age to the Information Age. With the launching of the railroads and mass production, we saw huge wealth creation in the 50 years following the Civil War. Barons were created—you know the names: Rockefeller, Mellon, Vanderbilt, Ford, Edison. These few select leaders created dynasties by generating millions of jobs for mostly factory workers. In fact, entire cities like Detroit and Pittsburgh, for example, only exist today because a business tycoon set up shop there. These leaders dictated salaries, owned the banks that lent money for local housing, and also built that housing. For many, a factory job was a dream come true: No more long hours in the fields with little pay. Now they could live in a city or town and work and chat side by side with people creating useful and cutting-edge widgets. This signaled major progress for the masses."

Cory shifted in his seat. *Where was this going?* he wondered.

Big Eye continued. "Then came the Information Age around World War II, when the phone, radio, and television became mainstream and people became much more informed. The 1960 presidential campaign began the practice of a televised formal debate—the first time millions of people got to see their candidates live and in action. Many historians claim that JFK won the election because he looked more clean-cut and trustworthy than Nixon did, with his five o'clock shadow. A few decades later, the Information Age really took off in the late 1990s with the World Wide Web. Today, we rely on search engines and have endless sources for research at our fingertips."

True story, Cory thought, glancing around the room. Everyone he could see had a cell phone at the ready, either in their hands, on their laps, or peeking out of their bags on the floor.

"Another example of a misunderstood market is the department store concept. For hundreds of years, local merchants sold one or two specific items. Back then, when you needed shoes, you bought them from the shoemaker, who custom-made your shoes within a few days or weeks. If you needed a new dress, you went to the dressmaker. For a hammer and some nails, you went to the local hardware shop. Customers received great, personal service. Then, in the late 1800s, along came Frank Woolworth, who had a new idea for the distribution of goods. He combined all the products and services of these local merchants into one big store with different departments and called it a 'department store.' Crazy! You weren't going to get customized service; you were going to have to pick out your shoes and try them on yourself.

That seemed a bit ridiculous, at the time. And how could anyone buy a dress that was already made? It would never fit!"

The audience chuckled as Big Eye paused to take a sip from his water bottle.

"Well, the department store concept started to take off, and then it went from being called ridiculous to being vehemently opposed. The merchants got together and tried to pass legislation declaring the department store idea illegal. That's how angry people were. However, any sharp businessperson could see it wouldn't be deemed illegal for long, if indeed it ever could be. Why? Because it was working! People were getting what they needed at better prices, and Woolworth was making money, too. You might call this concept free enterprise, evolution, or ingenuity. How could this be a bad thing? As you know, Woolworth's became one of the greatest stories in U.S. history. In fact, the empire grew so big that in 1910, Woolworth commissioned the construction of the tallest building in the world, located in downtown New York City, and paid the entire amount in cash. Construction was completed in 1913 and it remained the tallest building in the world until the Empire State Building took the title in the 1930s.

"Woolworth changed the world 100 years ago. Who else, in modern times, has changed the world, and changed the way we think? One of the first who comes to mind is Bill Gates, with his innovative software. Steve Jobs was another one—the main driver behind smartphones and proponent of having a computer in your pocket. Today, I would think of Elon Musk, who created PayPal and then sold it to make a fortune. Now he's into rockets and fast cars, and most recently, the solar industry. He asks the question,

'The sun is shining every day: Why can't we power the world with the sun?' I wouldn't bet against him. Imagine being ahead of the curve. These people really do change the world."

Ah, Cory could see where this was going, now. He could tell Big Eye was winding up, and ready to make his final points.

Big Eye took the microphone out of the stand and walked down to the front of the crowd.

"Network marketing has been around for decades. But today is the time to get involved. Be in front of the trend, don't be behind it. The change is happening now. Network marketing is thriving now more than ever. It's simply a distribution channel—a way to get a product or service to the people who want to consume it. The most productive network marketers make the most money, just like any other business model. They sell more products by teaching others how to do the same. If they're selling a decent product or service and the system is sound, it's a win-win-win," Big Eye said. "For example, my good friend Scott built a highly successful career with a network marketing company, and has helped thousands of others build their own organizations. I knew him only casually at first. When I found out what he did for a living—a nice living at that—I looked at him a little differently. He was one of those guys who made network marketing work for him. I tried that same company years before I met Scott but, as many of you know, I quit too soon because the timing wasn't right. Now here's Scott, who's been at it for over 20 years. He sets his own hours, inspires others, helps his clients reach their financial goals, and has built a residual income. He commanded my respect. He'd endured all the nonsense 20 years before, with friends and family telling him to quit network marketing and get a 'real' job. But Scott never wavered, and now he's enjoying the fruits of his labor."

Cory felt Big Eye was speaking directly to him, even though the room was packed with more than 500 people.

Big Eye continued. "The phrase to 'think outside the box' has become somewhat cliché, but it's never been more important. If your goals are to have more money, freedom, and satisfaction in life, then focus on a business that will bring you residual income. With today's technologies, you can work from home if you choose, and still achieve whatever you aspire to. Some people make a few extra hundred dollars a month this way to help supplement their income, while others make many times more than they ever could with a traditional job. When do you decide to get out of time poverty, and that enough is enough? The mind is powerful enough that you can do it if you really want to. If you truly decide that you're going to do something—quit smoking, take off that 50 pounds—you can do it. The mind is more powerful than you know. People are afraid of their potential, they are afraid of what they can actually do. Even in a good way, people are afraid of what they are actually going to get done. It's not going to happen unless you have a breakthrough and make a decision."

Another murmur ran through the crowd, and Cory could see many in the audience nodding in agreement. And there was that phrase again—time poverty.

"With network marketing, the people who are 'judging' you may be holding you back," Big Eye said, making air quotes with the word judging. "You may have an extensive education, and they may be telling you you're too educated to do this—you're way too qualified to be prospecting leads or going to meetings. You may be thinking, I've paid my dues, studied hard, spent $400,000 on education. I shouldn't be in someone's kitchen following up on people who are 'less' than me."

Big Eye paused again, letting that thought settle with the audience.

"That mindset is definitely going to hold someone back in network marketing," he continued. "Until you get over yourself, you're not going to make a lot of money in network marketing. You may see the light but deep down, you may stop, hesitate, maybe when one of your colleagues says, '*What* are you *doing*? You're risking your reputation and your job. You're a high-end financial guy; what are you doing with some silly home-based business?' That mindset is holding a lot of people back. You have to decide that you are going to do the right thing in this new economy. There's no reason why you can't make a very comfortable living from that smartphone in your pocket or handbag."

Big Eye concluded with a dramatic, yet encouraging, statement: "There are more than 500 people here tonight. Congratulations for showing up and skipping that hot new reality TV show. Congratulations for having an open mind and at least trying something a little different. Congratulations for dreaming big again. Congratulations for seeing that so many others are winning and feeling that you can win at this too. But

> Until you get over yourself, you're not going to make a lot of money in network marketing.

here's something I know to be true. In the next six to 12 months, about 400 of you will quit this business. Sad, but true. It's the 80/20 rule. Eighty percent of you will come up with some good enough reason to just go back to the same old grind. Here's the question you need to ask yourself when your head hits that pillow tonight: *Is this the time I really make it work for me?*"

As Big Eye replaced the microphone, the audience erupted. Everyone stood, cheering and whistling. Big Eye was clearly a beloved part of this company. In fact, Cory didn't remember seeing anyone ever turning away from Big Eye or listening with anything other than rapt attention. Anyone could tell that Big Eye was genuinely interested in the well being of the people he helped every day.

Cory and Dave waited for the crowd to thin, and finally, had a chance to greet Big Eye.

"I always feel better after hearing you speak," Cory said. "The company is lucky—we're lucky, to have you on our team. Thank you for the message. I really needed that!"

"So did I," Dave said, shaking Big Eye's hand. "You just keep getting better!"

"Well thanks, guys," Big Eye said humbly. "I'm constantly looking for ways to get better. That's what this business has taught me—that I have to get better to be better in this business. And I'm looking forward to being better a year from today, too."

CHAPTER 7

A Corporate Prospect

The weather had turned again, but this time to spring. Children were playing soccer on the dry fields that were slowly greening up in the bright spring sun.

"Hey Cory!" His neighbor Nancy greeted him warmly. Her daughter was already out warming up on the field. Elizabeth dropped her bag on the sideline and sprinted out to join her team.

As the girls began their drills, warming up for the first scrimmage of the year, Nancy asked, "So what's new?"

Cory hesitated briefly, and then told her about his new business. When he said it was home-based, Nancy perked up.

"Wait, you can do this from home?" she asked.

"Sure!" Cory said. "I have a video on my phone. It's about five minutes. You want to take a look?"

Nancy glanced toward the field where the girls were still warming up. She didn't want to miss any of the first scrimmage, but there was still some time before the game would begin.

"Sure," she said. "I've just been thinking about going back to work full-time. The partners in my firm offered me my old position, and quite a raise. But I'm just not sure I'm ready to leave my family at home alone after school just yet. The more I'm home, the more I think it's actually more important to be home with teenagers than with toddlers."

"I know!" Cory said. "We are finding the same thing. Boy, this is going to make so much sense to you!"

He clicked on the video and handed Nancy the phone. She slipped her earbuds on. Her eyes widened as the piece about opportunity played.

"This is cool, Cory!" she said loudly, the earbuds still in. He laughed and tapped his ears.

Just then, the shrill whistle beckoned the girls to their places on the field. "Hey, it looks like the game is starting. Thanks." Nancy popped out her earbuds, handed the phone back to Cory and turned to watch the game.

Deflated again, Cory turned to the game. He had wanted to get Dave on a call to talk to Nancy about the business. He would have to work on his timing.

But Cory's spirits didn't sag for long. Elizabeth was the lead scorer on the team, and she obviously hadn't lost any moves over the winter break. He loved watching his daughter play soccer. She never stopped working hard to improve. Elizabeth scored two goals, and both girls were elated when the game ended.

As the girls gathered their gear bags, Nancy said quickly, "Oh, Cory—that video. I'd like to know more about your company. How can I find out more? Can you send me the website so I can look into it over the weekend?"

"I'd rather get together in person. Let's meet tomorrow morning at that new café on Main," Cory suggested. "If you come a little early we can see the rest of the video and call Dave or his partner, Big Eye. You remember Dave? He used to own his own plumbing business."

"Oh Dave? I do remember him. Great!" Nancy agreed. "See you tomorrow."

CHAPTER 8

Gaining Momentum

It was a beautiful morning, and Cory chose a spot at a small table set back from the sidewalk on the flagstone patio. As Nancy approached, Cory waved her over.

"Outside OK?" he called.

"This is great!" Nancy said. "I love spring! After our winters, it's like coming alive again. And I've wanted to try this place. Thanks for inviting me! So this person we're going to listen to—what's with the nickname? The Big Guy? Is it because he's really tall? Or because he's successful in business? Or what?"

Cory laughed. "I'm not sure, but he's not a super tall guy. I also thought it was 'big guy,' but his nickname is actually 'Big Eye.'" Cory pointed to his eye. "I heard one guy say it's because he has an eye for talent, that he can see and bring out the best in people. Or that he's kind of a visionary—I'm not really sure."

He shrugged as the waiter arrived and they ordered coffee and a light breakfast.

Big Eye had a conference call scheduled for this morning, and Cory wanted to make sure he showed Nancy the video and made the three-way call to Dave with plenty of time.

Cory knew the call would start precisely on time, and quickly invited Nancy to see the rest of the video. He reminded her they would make a quick phone call to Dave so he could answer any questions. Cory was excited, as she was clearly interested! Nancy was one of the best attorneys at her firm, and even after leaving to work part-time from home while she raised her children, she was still regularly sought after by corporate headhunters. Her skills were sharp and people naturally gravitated to her; she was warm, and sincerely interested in others.

As the video ended, Cory quickly dialed Dave's number. Dave was expecting the call and picked up on the second ring.

"Nancy, nice to meet you!" Dave said. "Cory said you've seen the video and you might have some questions about our company?"

Nancy explained that she was a partner in a law firm in the city. Her dream had been to get into law school and do just what she had done—become a partner. Her specialty was business law and she loved helping business owners. She loved entrepreneurs and she loved helping people start things.

Things changed for her quite a few years ago, though; when the kids came along, she wanted to stay home with them. Now that her kids were in school, she still wanted to be home when they walked in the door.

"I actually think they need me more now, as teenagers, than they did when they were young," Nancy said. "I work with clients during the day, while the kids are in school, and I leave my afternoons open for the kids. It's been a great blend for me. But I am really interested in what Cory was explaining—residual income. Right now I help business owners, which I truly love. But I am trading my time and expertise for fees. So there's no 'do it once and it repeats' residual income. I just do the same thing over and over. It gets a little tiresome. I could use a new challenge! But I really do love helping business people. I love my clients."

"I'll make a suggestion," Dave said. "What if you ask me all of your questions, lay out your concerns about the business, and we'll go from there."

Nancy expressed almost the same concerns that Cory had: What would her parents think? How could she approach her clients? What would her clients say? Would they think she was desperate, maybe think that her husband Jeff had lost his job and suddenly she had to grovel for income?

"Same concerns I had, Nancy," Cory smiled. "I had some setbacks, but I'm learning to ignore the negativity."

"Cory's right," Dave said. "But it's not easy to ignore. Some people have really strong negative feelings about network marketing. Some eventually see the big picture and some don't. It's easier for the people who are already successful in business or another profession—like you are—to eventually see the potential.

> It's easier for the people who are already successful in business or another profession—like you are—to eventually see the potential.

So don't be afraid to approach them. There's a reason they're already successful—these are people who are open to getting better. They've led normal lives, and want advice from other 'normal' people. As I told Cory, no one is going to shoot you. You will hear plenty of people tell you no. And that's okay—having someone say 'no' won't kill you."

Nancy was nodding, but realized Dave couldn't see her and quickly answered, "True enough!" Since the business-building call was about to begin, they hung up with Dave and dialed into the other call.

As they connected, Big Eye was inviting people to give their name and say where they were calling from. A chorus of eager voices called out, most not recognizable in the onslaught.

"Wow!" Nancy said.

"Yep, there are probably a thousand or more people on this call," Cory said.

Big Eye muted the callers, greeted his audience, and began. "A lot of you were at the opportunity meeting where I talked about how things change in the world, and come to be an accepted practice. I want to talk to you today about how I was first introduced to network marketing by someone I really respected and admired."

Nancy leaned a little closer to the phone. The noise on the street was picking up, so Cory turned up the speaker.

"Most of you know I started my career on Wall Street. After 20 years of work, 10 years on Wall Street and 10 years as an owner of a brick-and-mortar business, one of my close friends and mentors made an appointment with me, to show me an opportunity. I was excited to meet with him! I thought he was going to show me a traditional business, maybe a partnership in a firm. But when we met, he explained to me that he was looking for something different to change his life. And then it dawned on him, he said: Network marketing was the answer! I remember feeling so deflated for him, so disappointed. We went through the presentation, and he gave me a DVD to watch. I promised to watch it. But I didn't watch it, which is really unlike me. I think I really just wanted to forget the whole thing. This guy who had been up on a pedestal for me was doing some 'desperate' stuff, in my eyes. He called and asked if I watched the DVD, and I told him I'd forgotten. He was so disappointed. I remember saying to him, emphatically, 'Listen, I will *never* do network marketing.' He went silent. I went on to tell him, I've just seen too many bad things happen. People lose their friends. It's just not for me. I will never be that guy who chases people to 'show them a business opportunity.' "

Big Eye paused and chuckled lightly. "It just goes to show you it's all about timing. Now, I'm not saying I regret my education or the hard years I put in on Wall Street. That diploma made me a lot of money in the first 20 years of my career. But it took a while for me to realize that piece of paper hanging in my den may actually be costing me millions of dollars and a sweet lifestyle going forward because I couldn't get past it. My point is this: If people don't have the right mindset, they won't understand the big picture. I know this because about a year later, the timing was right for me. I called this mentor, and I told him, 'Hey! Guess what? I'm in network marketing and I'd like you to take a look!' Guess what he said?"

Cory and Nancy laughed out loud as Big Eye paused for dramatic effect.

"You're right. 'Screw you,' he said. 'I thought you said you'd never do network marketing.' For months he wouldn't meet with me. I didn't let it stop me, and just plowed ahead, showing the business plan to all my other contacts. But it's all about timing. Two things at that time made a difference for me. My traditional business, which was centered on real estate, had really slowed down, and I needed some extra income. Actually, I needed a business where I could make unlimited income. And technology was getting better. Technology is really propelling this profession right now. Everyone now has fast Wi-Fi connections. It's not a big deal to do a presentation wherever you happen to be. Imagine that happening even a few years ago! It wouldn't," Big Eye said.

"So here's the lesson today," Big Eye concluded. "Don't give people a pass just because they don't have the right mindset today. Let them see the light in their own time. Just keep 'dripping' on them, and keep your belief in yourself."

Signing off, Big Eye reminded everyone on the call that there was an opportunity meeting next weekend, and to log on and make reservations, as it was already starting to fill up.

Now Nancy was really excited about the opportunity, and anxious to know more about the business.

"Let me see that video one more time," she said.

Cory tapped his phone to start the video. They hadn't brought headphones, but they were still nearly the only ones on the patio. It was early, and the lunch rush hadn't yet begun, so Cory cranked up the volume and handed his phone to Nancy.

The wait staff had just started circulating throughout the restaurant, offering the early lunch crowd some samples of a special pastry that was being rolled out that day.

"Hey—Nancy? Cory?"

Nancy and Cory turned to see one of their neighbors carrying a tray through the restaurant. "Oh, hi Milo!" Nancy said, as Cory turned down the volume a touch and paused the video.

"This is our new place!" Milo said.

"I thought your restaurant was in the city," Nancy said.

"It was—is," Milo said. "We just expanded. Rebecca wants to handle this location so she can be home when Nicole gets home from school."

"We saw Nicole at the game, but we didn't see you guys," Cory said. "We were hoping you weren't sick or something."

"No, just swamped. This place has sucked up all of our time, free and otherwise," Milo said. He gestured to Cory's phone. "Soccer video, I hope?" he asked. "I really hate missing games!"

"No, this is Cory's new business," Nancy said.

"You quit Wall Street?" Milo asked, incredulous.

"No, just trying out something new on the side," Cory said.

Milo leaned over to watch. "Here, I'll start it over. You don't mind, Nancy?" Cory asked. Nancy shook her head, and Milo took a chair from an adjoining vacant table and watched the video with them.

"That looks cool!" he said. He gestured to his wife, who was circulating with another platter of pastries nearby, and called, "Hey Rebecca, come take a look at this."

Cory restarted the video, and propped his phone in the center of the table so Milo, Rebecca, and Nancy could watch it all the way through.

When the video was done, Rebecca leaned back in her chair.

"I'd like just one day not worrying about the wait staff or cooks showing up," she said.

"Or having food inspectors who do show up—unexpectedly," Milo grinned.

Their restaurant was spotless, so obviously that would never be a problem.

"What sort of time commitment would we be looking at?" Rebecca asked.

Cory was already redialing Dave for a three-way call.

"Hang on," Cory said. "Dave is one of my business partners. He can answer any questions you have."

As Dave answered, Cory put the phone on speaker again and introduced his neighbors, who asked Dave to explain more about the opportunity and time commitment.

When they finished the three-way call, Milo and Rebecca were clearly impressed.

"Our group leader is giving a presentation this Tuesday night, but it's an hour away," Cory said. "You should really come though, because this guy Big Eye really adds a good perspective on this business."

"It's an hour away? I can drive an hour on a Tuesday night if this business is going to change my life as much as I am starting to think it is," Rebecca said.

Milo quickly agreed, and headed over to the bar to ask the manager if he could handle Tuesday evening at the restaurant on his own.

Cory was impressed. Milo and Rebecca were obviously serious businesspeople!

CHAPTER 9

Opportunity is Everywhere

Milo, Rebecca, Nancy, and Cory arrived early for the opportunity meeting. As was his custom, Big Eye was visiting with people throughout the room. Cory led his friends over to meet Big Eye, and then claimed the spots he had staked out near the front of the room.

This time, Big Eye had a computer, and he flashed a slide on the screen.

"I am not going to show you an entire presentation on this screen," he began. "But I want you to meet my cousin, Vito."

The slide showed a photo of a distinguished older Italian man with his arm around Big Eye. They stood in front of a Tuscan garden, with flowers in bright red pots hanging on a gate. Big Eye had captioned the photo, "*Opportunity Is Everywhere.*"

"Let me tell you a story," Big Eye began. "Whenever I talk about opportunity, I like to tell people about my cousin Vito, who moved to America with nothing as a young man, and left a self-made millionaire. In our business, people talk about opportunity. A lot. Here, let me show you *this* opportunity. Let me show you *that* opportunity. And then they draw a bunch of circles on the whiteboard."

Everyone in the room laughed, having been either the artist or audience for the circles.

Big Eye continued. "But the thing is, these really *are* opportunities. People often don't realize the wonder of this era we are living in. Let me tell you a story about how I learned to really value every opportunity, and really, how I learned to create my own. It's what allowed me to see the gift my friend was sharing when he told me about the opportunity in our company."

Big Eye took the microphone from the stand and walked across the stage, surveying both sides of the room.

"After World War II, our country was in one of its most prosperous times. Not everyone realized it at the time. But it was a huge economic growth spurt. It's always been true, but particularly during this time, there was a large influx of immigrants who came to this country and became self-made millionaires. I was lucky enough to have one of them as my cousin Vito. Now, a lot of people speculate as to why immigrants are so much more likely to become self-made millionaires. Is it because Americans are born with opportunity, and don't see it as readily? Is it because many of these immigrants come from abject poverty, and are desperately moved to improve their lives? When people come from such a place of depression, they don't see the time they're in as 'too late.' They see it as a huge opportunity. They ask, 'How can I make the most of this opportunity, this gift I am being presented?'

"They embrace the language, and learn the customs, business practices, and tax laws of this country. They have to work a little harder to find their way in a country where everything is new. There's opportunity everywhere. It's all about your mindset. Do you see it, or do you not see it? Did you get in late or early? It doesn't really matter. Opportunity is always there. The people who grow are the people who are going to make it."

Big Eye crossed the stage again, and gestured to the slide. "Anyway, about my cousin Vito. I saw his story unfold before my eyes throughout my life and it's always inspired me. He's been a mentor to many, although he didn't intend to be. My mother comes from a close family in Italy. Her father, my grandfather John, is the classic story of an immigrant traveling on a boat to Ellis Island, New York, in the early 1900s, to build a dream. He arrived in this country in 1919 at the age of 18 with less than a dollar in his pocket. He moved in with his brother Michael, who had come a few years earlier, and stayed until he could get a job and a place of his own. John soon started his own business delivering ice in the summer and coal in the winter. Most of the Italians that came from Bari, Italy, worked in this field. No one knows exactly how they were drawn to this specific field of work. A few of their friends and family probably were hired by a local business, and they simply started recruiting each other when they saw the great demand for ice and coal.

"Anyway, John then got married, had four children—the youngest, my mother Claire—and lived a respectable, fulfilling life. Never rich, never poor, he was a proud man who truly loved America and the opportunity it afforded him and his family.

Think about these Italian immigrants from 100 years ago. It must have been quite intimidating leaving a home where you were safe and secure. No one was starving because they always had plenty of food living in such a fertile farming region. They didn't have CNN, MTV, or the Internet showing off the American lifestyle and the 'land of opportunity.' The success stories all came by word of mouth across the Atlantic. These Italians were safe and secure in their own country but had little chance to ever get ahead in life. They could barely read or write Italian, let alone English. And of course, Italians are known for having very close family ties. Most of them left for America knowing full well they would most likely never see their parents and friends ever again. Yet some, not all, took the plunge.

"Of course my grandfather's story was special to me, but his story was shared by millions. You'll find lots of these stories of people emigrating from all parts of Europe back in the early 20th century. Even today, people want to get into the United States and make a better life for themselves and their families. I wonder what these people must murmur under their breath when they hear about someone born in the U.S. with a decent education who is still struggling to make ends meet?"

Gesturing again to the photo of Vito, Big Eye smiled and said, "But I digress!" The audience chuckled, obviously fans of his storytelling.

"Vito was my grandfather's nephew, son of his brother Pasquale, who never made the journey to America. Pasquale was happy to stay in Italy, and he lived a good, long life there. But Vito came to America in the late 1950s, when he was in his early

20s, and moved in with my grandfather until he could get on his feet. A short, stout, powerfully built man, Vito always promised anyone who hired him that he would do the work of two men. He was always trying to show his value. Whenever he saw two men loading bags of cement sand, he would insist on lifting the bags all by himself. To use his term, he worked like a 'jackass.' "

Laughter rippled through the room, and Big Eye smiled.

"Every time he used that term, I had to chuckle. I think something was lost—or perhaps added—in the translation. I think he meant to say 'mule,' as in a hardworking animal that did all the heavy lifting. However, 'jackass' also hints to that burning feeling inside that he knew he was better than that. He knew he had more in store for his immediate future, but he had to pay his dues. He planned to leave the grunt work to the people with no dreams. So here was Vito, age 24, a basic laborer who didn't speak English, who knew deep down he was born for a better life. Although he wasn't very educated, he had a great understanding of what he needed to do to become successful. He surely hadn't read any of Napoleon Hill's work, and Anthony Robbins wasn't even born yet. Where was his drive coming from? What skills did he have to organize his plan and follow through? It had to be innate. His own father had opted to stay in Italy and pass up on the land of opportunity, yet some of his brothers and his son couldn't resist pursuing opportunity in another country. I often wonder how I would fare if I were put into a situation like Vito's? What if I were plopped into a city in the middle of China? How well would I do? China is a great example of a booming economy with a huge economic future similar to that of the U.S. in the early

20th century. Think about the hurdles and the challenges—a new language, new rules, and no contacts. Yet millionaires are being created every day in China. The opportunity is limitless. It makes you think about what we have here in America."

"I've never thought about that," Nancy whispered to the others.

"Every success story starts with a plan," Big Eye continued. "But did Vito write down his goals the way you and I do? Did he have specific written goals with timelines and dates? Short-term and long-term goals taped to his mirror where he could see them every morning when he was shaving? You know, the stuff we've been hearing all our lives—the strategies that have been proven to work so well?"

Big Eye answered his own question. "No. Vito didn't even know there was a science to becoming successful. But he had something perhaps even more powerful than written goals. Vito had a clear, obsessive vision of what he wanted and where he wanted to be. This steady vision pulsated in his mind constantly as he labored 10 to 11 hours a day digging ditches or laying brick in all types of weather. While he was driving to work, he wasn't thinking about checking his email or how his sports team did last night. He wasn't looking forward to attending the cocktail party this weekend or playing around on Facebook, and he wasn't dreaming of buying a new car or taking a vacation he couldn't afford.

"No. He was thinking of where he wanted to be and what he had to do in that moment to get closer to his goal of owning his own business and having people work for him. Think of how exhausting it must have been for Vito to persevere without knowing any of the success techniques such as simply writing your goals down. I'm not advising you to become obsessive with your goals like Vito. He had to obsess about his goals because that's all he knew. For you and me it can be easier. I tell people to just write your goals down. Just do it. Keep them in your pocket and read them two to three times a day. Having written goals is crucial to success. Yet most people still just won't do it.

"Anyway, Vito became laser focused on his boss. Vito wanted to own and run his own business just like him, but even better. That was his big goal, so he studied his boss. He thought, *What makes this boss so special? Why do I have to get dirty and sweaty every day and he doesn't? Why does he get to drive a nice new air-conditioned truck from job to job and never break a sweat? Why does he get to decide who works today and who goes home? Why does he get to decide how much profit margin to build in on his price quotes? How did he get into a position to have twelve thankful 'jackasses' working for him?*"

At the mention of "jackasses," laughter rippled across the audience again.

"This is what Vito was thinking, not in a vindictive way, but in a healthy, positive way. He wasn't jealous so much as he was in awe. He wanted to be like his boss, but even better. He wanted to treat his employees better than his boss was treating him and his co-workers. He wanted to pay them more, to use higher quality materials, to create 'masterpieces' and have word get out that the best mason in town had finally arrived. These were some of his short-term goals, the fastest way to secure a financial future for himself and his family. Could Vito have gone back to school? Could he have learned perfect English, received his GED, enrolled in a local community college, gotten straight As, and transferred into a prestigious academic institution? Maybe. Or, he could just focus and work hard to accomplish his dream. He decided to run with what he knew best. Simply learn from those around him, always work hard, always be supportive and helpful, always show up on time, do what he said he was going to do every time. Be trustworthy and reliable, and become a leader, a magnet that attracts other quality people in his laborers' world.

"Vito soon started getting a few of his own projects on weekends and at night. His hard work earned him the notice from his peers, and people trusted him to follow through. He recruited coworkers to follow him and work for him for extra pay. They trusted him. Vito was emerging as a leader, as a potential new boss for people who admired him. Often, people in this line of work would get into jobs that they couldn't finish, or they'd run out of money and not pay their workers. So while working an extra five hours a night for someone new was often viewed as risky, people trusted Vito and were drawn to him. This was new territory for him, but he acted the part and kept forging ahead. The visions he'd been focusing on so clearly were becoming a reality. Was he excited? Was he surprised? Not really. Everything was going according to plan! If you truly believe in your goals and your destiny, you'll find that you don't get excited when you arrive because it feels normal. You expected it. This is a good thing. It means you're growing."

Big Eye had crossed back over to the side of the room where Cory and the others sat. He smiled at their group, took a sip from his water bottle, and continued.

"In just a few short years after he'd arrived in America, Vito had a thriving business all to himself. He had a new truck and he didn't have to get sweaty and dirty—although he still did from time to time to show what hard work is all about. He always delivered exactly as promised and a little more, whereas his competition always seemed to be late and sloppy. He'd gone from 'jackass' to boss. Mission accomplished, yes? Vito had just turned the corner in the masonry/construction business. But Vito didn't stop there. Vito was all about building a team and taking people along for the ride. One of nine siblings, he sent for a few of his brothers from Italy to come help him. But he didn't play favorites. Some of his brothers were hard workers and some were just okay, and Vito had no problem promoting a stranger over a brother if he earned it.

"One day Vito's brother Michael approached him with another opportunity. Hmmmm, sound familiar?" Big Eye asked. The crowd laughed.

"Michael wanted Vito to check out his business plan and perhaps partner with him to buy a fledging little bakery. His brother wanted to convert it to a commercial bakery, specifically to bake bread for local stores and restaurants. Now, Vito's business was booming. He had too much work to handle as it was, and he was making more money than he'd planned. He didn't need to start a bakery! He could live a comfortable life and be yet another nice success story. But not Vito. He realized he had a gift of some sort, and he had a large extended family. He wanted to bring more people up with him."

Here, Big Eye clicked to show another slide, this one of a beautiful Italian city. "The town that Vito and my grandfather come from is called Altamura, also known as 'Città del Pane,' or 'City of Bread.' In fact, you'll see signs on the highway as you enter town, touting the town's famous bread. Altamura is a small, ancient town, about a 30-minute drive west of the port town of Bari on the southeast part of the boot-shaped peninsula. Ask any Italian where the best bread comes from, and the answer is always Altamura. Just as you could ask any American where the best cheesesteaks or crab cakes come from and the answers would be Philly and Maryland, respectively.

"So Vito's brother Michael suggested that New York City had a need for the world's greatest bread. Part of the idea came from the simple fact that he was homesick for a decent loaf himself! In addition, numerous owners of fine Italian restaurants knew good bread when they tasted it, and would surely try a product baked by natives of the legendary Altamura. Therefore, the plan was to somehow recreate the same Altamura-type bread and build another successful business. Vito knew this would diversify his income and give him even more leverage. Plus, the oven would do a lot of the work for him!"

Big Eye clicked back to the slide of his cousin.

"Now, Vito had come from the bread capital of Europe, but he'd never baked a loaf in his life. He didn't have any bakery knowledge, but he now knew he could do whatever he set his mind to. Vito agreed to start the bakery business with his brother

Michael because he saw an opportunity to bake loaves of bread for pennies and sell them for dollars, while still managing his thriving construction business. In addition, this was a way to invite more of his family and friends to ride his wave of success. Successful people know that taking advantage of others or stomping on people to get ahead is a fool's game, whereas bringing people up with them spreads the wealth and helps the whole community."

While he always spoke with great emotion, Big Eye infused this last sentence with an intensity that silenced the crowd.

"When Vito told me this story, of how he started the bakery, he kept saying in broken English, 'I want to be big!' It always made me laugh, because he is such a short man. But he was so emotional about his desire to be BIG. Of course I knew exactly what he meant. He wanted to build a big business, not grow a foot taller, and the intensity of his desire to grow helped him achieve his goal. A lot of people would spend

> Successful people know that taking advantage of others or stomping on people to get ahead is a fool's game, whereas bringing people up with them spreads the wealth and helps the whole community.

time writing down a business plan. By what date would he be open? How many sales would he have his first month, his first six months? Where would he like to be in a year? But again, he had all this in his head and was living and breathing it 24/7. He didn't need goals on paper to remind him. What worked for him was to just go for it. And, we have to remember, he had the help of a small village—his family."

At this, Milo elbowed Rebecca playfully, and reached over to take her hand.

"This is cool, Cory," Milo whispered. Rebecca was smiling widely, and nodded her agreement.

"Well, Vito's bakery did become big. It sold bread and then gourmet packaged cookies to all the fine restaurants and delicatessens throughout the New York metro area. Vito's next plan was to return home to Altamura with $500,000 in cash. This was a small fortune back in the late 1960s when you could buy a fine four-bedroom home for $30,000. He mentioned this goal to one of his American cousins and she laughed. That was a crazy amount of money to her.

"Why back to Italy? Wasn't America the land of opportunity? Vito had left southern Italy because the economy had become stagnant and there wasn't much demand for his work. Now he had a wildly successful bakery and all the finer things in life in the great land of America. He also had four daughters who were all American citizens. Why sell? Why leave? Having recently returned from Italy myself, I can see why people might like to live there, especially if it's your hometown; the weather, the food, the people, the *dolce vita* lifestyle—all good."

Big Eye nodded and patted his stomach for emphasis, bringing the audience to laughter again. No paunch there! It was clear this guy had time to work out.

"So Vito returned to his hometown of Altamura after 15 years in the United States with a lot more than the $500,000 he'd planned on bringing back. In fact, he returned a legitimate millionaire in the 1970s. The journey that took him from digging ditches to millionaire in 15 years was worth more to him than an Ivy League MBA. But he didn't exactly rest on his laurels. Not Vito! Taking his sleepy town by storm, Vito quickly bought land and built apartment and condo complexes. Leveraging his money and his reputation to build an even greater empire, he hired hundreds of people and built much-needed affordable housing. He'd learned a lot about how business works by being an entrepreneur and he lit up his hometown, showing the not-so-motivated townspeople how to make things happen for them. He became a true leader and an inspiration for Altamura, Italy, which today is a thriving and charming metropolis."

Big Eye flipped back to the first slide of him with his cousin. "Vito is now close to 80 years old, but he looks about 15 years younger. He is fit and relaxed. When we visited a few years ago, he loved showing us, his American family, around the town he helped build. He's still building today! He showed us which cranes soaring in the sky were his. He then took us out to the finest restaurants with his entire extended family. Vito was very proud to hear I was doing so well, even though I'm not really sure he really understood my business."

Big Eye switched off the computer and moved to the center of the stage, looking out over the crowd.

"So here's the bottom line, folks. If a barely educated laborer from another country with no formal sales skills or training can live out his dream, why can't we all? Success in this business has nothing to do with your education level, where you came from, your investment portfolio, or anything else. In this business, belief matters more than anything else. It's not a get-rich-quick scheme—don't get confused about that. It's hard work, make no mistake. You're not out to rise above everyone else, but to bring as many people up with you as possible."

As Big Eye ended his presentation, Milo said, "Wow, that was more than worth the one-hour drive over here!" Leaning over to Rebecca, he inquired, "Babe?"

"I'm in if you are," Rebecca answered.

Milo turned to Cory and Nancy, who was already all-in. "OK team. Let's do this!"

CHAPTER 10

The Entrepreneurs Dig In

As it turned out, Rebecca wanted to see the video one more time. They all met at the restaurant the morning after the opportunity meeting. Milo and Rebecca had a couple of hours before customers would begin arriving for lunch, and the prep staff was busy in the kitchen.

After the video, Cory dialed Big Eye for a three-way call, since Dave was out of the country on a mission trip. Cory reintroduced Milo and Rebecca to Big Eye.

"What questions do you guys have?" Big Eye began.

"We've always owned restaurants," Rebecca said. "We didn't start with this one—our first location is in the city. It's all we've ever done. It's great, but there are so many things to do every day." She glanced toward the kitchen, where the prep staff, short a member, was getting everything ready for lunch. "You never know what any given day is going to bring. We could come in some morning to find all the power has been out overnight and all of the food in the refrigerators spoiled. Or our wait staff could call in sick. We're a small place, and deeply involved every day. It seems we do the same thing, over and over again. The money is great, but the repetition…" Rebecca trailed off.

"Ah, I'm well aware of the problems you face with a brick and mortar business," Big Eye said. "I explained to Cory and Nancy that I did start my own traditional business after leaving Wall Street. Two of them actually! The first one was just crazy risky. I leveraged my house, had two kids in diapers. It wouldn't have worked without the cooperation of an extremely supportive spouse. We almost went broke, but we did whatever it took to make it work. And it did! I eventually sold my ownership in that business. Afterward, I was introduced to network marketing but, believe it or not, I still didn't take the plunge. I started yet another traditional business that took a nosedive when the market crashed in 2008. But I still own that one and I have some great people who run it for me. But that's also when I found the right opportunity in network marketing. And the timing was right. You just have to be ready to embrace the opportunity."

"We often work for lower pay, seven days a week, 12 to 14 hours a day," Milo said. "We have to manage the staff, do all the buying, create the recipes. We keep thinking the harder we work, the more we sacrifice, the more successful our restaurant will be."

"But really, it just leaves one of us to raise our daughter," Rebecca chimed in. "I would actually be OK with that, and that alone, without the worry of the restaurant. But it's all we've ever done and I don't really know how to do any other business. It took us a lot of time to get our first restaurant up and running, so we are hoping this will be easier. But still—it's not residual. We have to do the same things over and over, every day."

"I understand that too," Big Eye remembered. "Our reality was stark for a while. We had no money coming in, and our two babies still needed food, clothing, diapers, and toys. We still had to buy some family birthday and holiday gifts, so we put vacations on hold. My wife could have gone back to work, but paying for full-time childcare wouldn't have made much sense. I had some savings socked away, but it was quickly evaporating."

Cory was sure he knew the story that was coming up, and he was right. Big Eye had shared this with him on an earlier call.

"When I left my Wall Street employer to strike out on my own, I'd taken over the company car lease, and the payments for the gorgeous Lexus were killing me," Big Eye said. "When the lease was up, I couldn't risk purchasing the car because I knew I might need that money soon to pay the mortgage. I had to give it up and find a much cheaper car to lease. So I leased a brand new, lime green Toyota Corolla for $99 a month. I guess the dealership couldn't get rid of it, so they cut me a great deal. So not only was this car not a Lexus, it was lime green! But it was safe and reliable. After some very stressful years, in the long run the business became profitable. After a while, I sold my interest in it to my partners, and used the money to build a nice five-bedroom home in a neighborhood with excellent schools. So it worked out rather well, in a way, but it sure was a long hard ride. Man, I wish I'd known more about home-based businesses back then."

"Once an entrepreneur, always an entrepreneur," Nancy interjected.

"That's true also," Big Eye said. "I've already told you about my next venture—it's the one I still own today. Success in the title insurance industry is all about service and relationships. We were successful until the housing boom crashed in late 2008, when the business almost came to a standstill. Once again, I'd gotten lured away from a business that was residual. One of my buddies kept hounding my business partner Frank and me to meet with him to see a business plan. He insisted on meeting in person. It was network marketing. But this time we leapt aboard, and we quickly became top producers in the business. We were finally realizing that this 'new' model of home-based business had some great legs. No overhead, no risk—it was the future. We learned a great deal about ourselves, how to motivate people, and to always keep our eyes and ears open for a high-potential opportunity. Plus, we understood that traditional business owners like us could be the future budding superstars in home-based businesses—if they could just 'see' it.

"We ended up switching to this company, which we felt had the best long-term fit for us. We were blown away by the potential of an untapped market converging right here in our backyard. The statistics were mind-boggling. This network marketing group had plans to spread into multiple states with similar attractive demographics. It was almost effortless for people to become customers. Now here was an opportunity!

"My business partner Frank and I jumped in 100 percent and quickly became one of the company's biggest producers. We're now regarded as being among the few top network marketing experts and earners in the world. Besides the monthly residual income, I've grown to love the low overhead and unlimited profits of the network marketing model. Before I'd taken another serious look at this business model, I didn't realize you could truly make millions of dollars a year while helping others. I've seen a new trend developing. Traditional business owners with employees, long leases, insurance, and other such limitations are now flocking to quality network marketing businesses."

As Big Eye paused, Milo said softly, "I know we are. It almost sounds too good to be true."

Big Eye answered quickly. "Milo, my advice to traditional entrepreneurs is simple: If you're the type of person who always finds yourself in the top five to ten percent of your field, then get involved with a quality network marketing company. Most business owners tire quickly of the aggravation of running a typical business. And even if you handed me a successful franchise for free, I'd politely decline. You could offer me a business worth $1 million with a proven track record on a busy corner, and I would rather stick with my network marketing business."

Milo looked at Rebecca, who was nodding, and then to Nancy and Cory. "Where do we sign up, and what's next?" he asked.

CHAPTER 11

Catching the Vision

Cory arrived early and snagged his favorite table in the corner overlooking the courtyard. This was one of his favorite spots in this entire town. In the spring, the tulips and daffodils peeked out from the bark and rocks covering the garden spot that ran between the tables and the street. After these intense winters, he really looked forward to this little burst of spring. He flipped open his laptop as he waited for Nancy. He'd have the video ready and waiting when she arrived with her prospect, and there would be plenty of time to call Dave before the weekly business-building call with Big Eye.

He was greeted with a graphic of his goals every time his computer was switched on, and Cory smiled as he remembered writing them. Had it only been four months ago that he'd begun this business?

One of the first things Big Eye had told him was this: "The very first step is identifying your *why*. Why are you doing this business? You might say, I'm doing this business to make money. But that's too vague. Why are you going to a meeting on Tuesday night in snow and sleet? Why are you going to go that extra mile? To put your kids through college? To move your parents closer to you? To get out of debt? Why are you doing this business?"

"To get the heck out of the rat race," Cory had responded wryly.

"Why do some people go for their master's degree at night— put in that extra 10 to 12 hours a week, pay extra tuition, and spend weekends doing homework and reports?" Big Eye had asked.

"To make themselves more marketable," Cory had said.

"It's the same in network marketing. You have to work hard. But more than that, you have to have conviction. Have a *why* that will make you cry. Otherwise, you may quit," Big Eye had said.

"Cory!" He looked up from his screen to see Nancy waving to him from across the courtyard. "We'll be right there," she called.

Nancy had run into Celia at the soccer game last night. They both knew Cory from soccer, and they both also knew Dave, who had contracted the plumbing at Celia and Don's house a few years ago. Nancy also told her about Cory, who had introduced her to this business and was thinking about stepping away from his Wall Street job, and about Milo and Rebecca, who were working the business as well as their new restaurant.

"And I'm going to do this business alongside my legal consulting," Nancy added. Tentatively, she'd asked if Celia might want to take a look, and when she said yes, she'd set up this meeting with Cory.

The two women greeted Cory and he pulled up the video while they waited for their coffee. After the video, Cory dialed

Dave, inviting Celia to ask him any questions she had about the business.

Celia, a corporate accountant and partner in her firm, brought up the same concerns the others had, but she was especially hung up on the training aspect. "I had to go through a lot of training to become an expert in my field, and I'm just afraid I won't have the time to become an expert in this business too," she said.

"You don't have to talk too much. In fact, you shouldn't," Dave said. "Just show the video. And then get on a three-way call with Nancy or Cory—or me. In network marketing the biggest obstacle we have is people don't feel they have enough time to do the business. They ask, can I do it, is it worth it, will it work for me? Because everyone is pressed for time, dedicated to making a living, we want people to really see the business model. A lot of people ask their prospects if they want to make extra money, or they ask about their retirement plan. Instead, you can just say, 'Hey I started a new business and I'd love for you to see my business plan. Can we meet for coffee? I want to get your opinion on my new venture.' Too many times people get all excited, talk too much, and scare others away. After most people see the business, the income opportunity will click. The important thing is to get them to see it."

> Hey I started a new business and I'd love for you to see my business plan. Can we meet for coffee? I want to get your opinion on my new venture.

"I don't usually carry a laptop," Celia interjected.

"Oh, you don't have to," Nancy answered. "Cory showed me

the video on his phone. At soccer! I watched it while the girls were warming up."

"Celia, your concern about having time to learn a new business is one of the biggest obstacles for a lot of people who would be great at network marketing. The thing is, you don't actually have to learn a whole industry," Dave said.

"So how do you answer all the questions?" Celia asked. "If someone came in and asked me to do their taxes, and I didn't know the answer to all of their detailed questions, I would be out of work!"

"If they like what they see on the video, and they see regular people making money at this, then of course they're going to be curious," Dave said. "They'll ask questions, some may already be answered in the video—maybe they weren't paying attention so remember, just be patient. Let them ask the questions, but you don't answer them. Remind them before the presentation starts that you're going to call one of your business partners after the video, someone who has been doing this longer than you have. You can even say, 'We're going to call this guy and try to poke some holes in this program. Ask him why you shouldn't be doing this business. Frankly I'm excited about it and I want to spend more time on it. I want to know if I'm nuts, if there's something I'm missing, something I'm not asking.' "

Dave added, "When people ask me today how much time I really spent during my first year doing this business, my answer is always the same: not enough! If I had worked just a little harder in the beginning my business could be exponentially bigger today."

"You can even invite them to give the person you call a hard time, right Dave?" Cory said. "Now the prospect feels more like an advisor, trying to poke holes and trying to save you a lot of time and frustration. We're just trying to show our business model to a sharp and successful person. This soft angle shows people you don't have to be an expert to start and grow this business. You can earn while you learn. I always call my third-party backup. If you sit there and answer every question like Mr. Smarty Pants, you're actually going to scare people away."

"Hey, Cory!" Dave said. "You've got it! Celia, it all comes down to fear. People who are interested in network marketing know it's better. But just like you, they don't think they have enough time to learn a whole new industry. We call someone else to be the expert and give the answers. If I'm the one showing the video, I shut up. All you have to do is show the video and make a phone call to a third party, who will answer the questions. You've shown someone the business model, but someone else is the expert. So they don't expect you to be an expert, and they see the chain of support you have in this business."

Celia still looked a little puzzled.

"What other questions do you have, Celia?" Cory said.

"I'm used to being an expert in my field, so this seems weird to me. In fact, everyone at my office feels compelled to be an expert," she said.

"In this business you *do* want to become an expert," Dave said. "But knowing that the single biggest obstacle is fear of lack of time to become an expert, it's important to show others that you don't have to be one. There's always someone upline, crossline, or on your team who can be the expert. That's why you always do a three-way call after showing the video. Why scare good people away by doing it the wrong way? It's not fair to you and definitely not fair to them. Hopefully this conference call has shown you that you may be in business for yourself, but you won't be in business by yourself. Help is always just a phone call away."

> Why scare good people away by doing it the wrong way? It's not fair to you and definitely not fair to them.

"It all sounds great! I still don't have any time," Celia said.

"That's what I thought too, Celia," Cory added quickly. "I still work full-time on Wall Street, but I found that if people really want to, they can always find 15 to 20 minutes per day to set up a conference call. I fit it in on my way home or during a break. Meanwhile, I am starting to build an income. Hopefully it will replace my full-time income someday. It's 15 to 20 minutes—like the time we just spent here!"

"I'm going to leave you with this thought, Celia," Dave said. "There are people not half as smart as you, not half as connected as you, not half as motivated as you, not half as successful as you, not half as talented as you, who are going to retire in the next three to five years—simply because they showed videos and made phone calls. You can do a three-way call from anywhere. If they don't want to join, you can just ask them if they know someone else who might be interested in showing videos and making phone calls. And then leave it at that."

"So I really don't have to do this alone? Even if I'm working out of my own house?" Celia was catching on.

"Everyone needs at least some training when starting anything new. Take any Fortune 500 CEO and stick him or her behind a cash register at a fast-food restaurant during a busy time of day with no training at all, and he or she will fail. Even though running a cash register isn't difficult, without at least 15 to 30 minutes of learning where the coded keys are and the basics on how to operate it, the results would be disastrous," Dave said.

They said their goodbyes and Cory dialed into the business-building call. Cory could tell Celia still was hesitant.

"Here's something that will really resonate for you, Celia," Cory said, while they were waiting for the call to begin. "Especially now, since tax time is over!"

"I wish it was," Celia said, rolling her eyes. "We always have the procrastinators. I'll be doing taxes all summer for these guys. It's the same ones every year."

"So when I first looked into this, I was all about the income potential," Cory said. "I figured I pay about half my income in taxes and other fees, and I work hard all the time. So when Big Eye explained the tax system for business owners I was all ears. As you well know, the tax system greatly favors the business owner, especially when compared to the W2 wage earner. So a home-based business owner may be able to take home a way higher percentage of his or her income. That was—and is—important to me."

Celia nodded and looked thoughtfully at the phone as the business-building call came on.

"Good morning everyone! Big Eye here, coming to you from Nicaragua this morning!"

Big Eye was out of the country on a mission trip. He did this every year, along with his top team-builders. As he had explained to Cory, and then later to Nancy, it was part of his *why*—he loved service and giving back.

"My call will be brief today, as we've just finished up our service project and arrived at our conference destination," Big Eye said. "But I wanted to take this opportunity to share part of my experience with you. Every time I talk to someone who is thinking about going into network marketing, I ask them, why? Why are you here? Why do you want to do this business? Knowing your *why* is a big part of your belief in network marketing. My *why* has changed. My *why* when I started in network marketing was simple. It was to get out of debt, and to feel good about the fact that I had to put three kids through college. We had some rough years in our traditional business, making payroll, having to let people go. We went into debt thinking that the mortgage business was going to come back, and it never really did. My first *why* was to get out of debt. And I did it. Now my *why* is to help people. My business partner and I decided once we got to where we were earning six figures a month we would go to the food bank and hand out food. So now we volunteer our time as well. Writing a check is easy. We show up and hand out food at the food shelter. That became part of my *why*. We also participate in a mission trip once a year, where we go to a remote area of the world and bring improvements to the locals—life-changing value they would never see if not for our help."

Big Eye paused for a few seconds, and then cleared his throat.

"So I wake up in the morning and pinch myself. I am financially secure. Now I am on a mission to help other people. I want everyone to know that not only can you get out of debt, this business can give you financial success. You can write bigger checks and spend more time with people who need it. That's what this business is all about. We are relentless with helping people. This business takes on a life of its own when you grow it the right way. Did you realize you could retire in five years? You're going to get paid residuals for decades. There's no way I could be on this mission trip, year after year, if I was still running a traditional business daily. Or if I was chained to my trading desk."

The line crackled a bit, and there was laughter in the background. "Time to go! Thanks for being on the call everyone," Big Eye said, signing off.

"Well, I'm definitely going to give this some more thought," Celia said. "Right now, though, I need to get to the office. Ready Nancy?"

"I'm going to have another cup of coffee," Nancy said. "I'll catch a ride home with Cory."

Nancy was bubbling with excitement as she told Cory about a conversation she'd had with a private legal client the day before. Her client had been with her for years, and owned a small business with several salespeople. She had simply asked him to watch the video with her and then poke holes in it, as a favor to her. Even though Nancy was already fully on board with the business for herself, she truly wanted her client's opinion before forging ahead with approaching the rest of her clients.

"I'm a lawyer," she'd said to her client. "You're an entrepreneur and businessman. Tell me what I'm missing here. This opportunity seems too good to be true."

After the video, since Cory was at work, Nancy had texted Dave, who was available for a three-way call.

Her client had set out to be critical, just as she had requested. But in the end he'd been impressed with the video, and with the answers Dave had provided. Nancy's client was going to try it out, and planned to show the business to all of his salespeople. Nancy specialized in law specific to small business owners, and she had a stable of steady clients, even though she had worked part-time from home for years. Now, Nancy told Cory, after this successful invitation, her plan was to show all of her clients this business.

Wow! Cory thought. *Nancy and Dave are working together, which grows **my** business while I am at work. They're growing my business, and I'm not even there! That's leverage.*

"You know, I never thought of myself as an entrepreneur," Nancy continued. "But I am, regardless of my degrees and the fact that I passed the bar. I've been working from home part-time since the kids were little. I don't know why I never thought of it before, but I truly am an entrepreneur. I'm going to show all of my clients the business. You will be getting a lot of three-way calls!"

"I'm ready any time," Cory said, raising his coffee cup in a salute. "And I'm so glad you're on my team!"

CHAPTER 12

Moment of Doubt

Cory logged into his back office and reclined as he admired his downline geneaology. Big Eye and Dave had been right! Once he put his head down and worked on his own mindset, people had flocked to his business. Nancy, in particular, was crushing it; her network marketing family dwarfed his. She had approached every one of her small business law clients, and many had joined her team. Several of those had even signed up their entire sales team, and her numbers were growing daily. Milo and Rebecca were not far behind Nancy. Cory had definitely found a couple of aces.

Milo and Rebecca had turned the day-to-day operations of the restaurants over to their longtime day managers, who had picked up the reins beautifully. Celia, unfortunately, had only signed up a few people before retreating to the comfort of her accounting office. And even though he was having great success building his business, Cory had been ultra careful to never, ever, mention network marketing around his Wall Street colleagues again. The incident at the lodge still burned, and a few of the less mature guys at the office still found ways to needle him.

Today, though, he was on the sideline of the soccer field once again. It was a gorgeous early fall day, following a glorious, productive summer. The high school fall soccer season had just begun, and Cory had taken the afternoon off to watch the first soccer scrimmage of the season.

Nancy, Cory, Milo, and Rebecca lounged in beach chairs on the sidelines, chatting amiably with the other parents who had turned into friends over the years that their children had played soccer together. Celia's husband Don joined them right before the game was set to begin.

"Hey Don," Nancy said as he unfolded his chair next to hers. "Is Celia coming?"

"Nope, she asked me to record the game for her," Don said, setting up a small tripod. "She has a tax mess with her biggest client, and she'll be grinding that out for a long time."

"Bummer," Cory said. "She'll be sorry to miss the game." He didn't bring up the business, and neither did Don. Celia had lost interest almost immediately, but Cory felt certain she would engage again someday.

Cory glanced back out at the field, and as his eye swept down the field he noticed a familiar figure setting up his chair at the end of the other parents' section.

Bill. He'd forgotten that Bill had a daughter this age, and he didn't know she played soccer. Across the field Bill spotted Cory at almost the same time, and waved. Surprised, Cory waved back. Then Bill formed a triangle—a pyramid—with his hands.

Cory's face flamed. "Oh man," he muttered, looking down.

"What?" Nancy asked, turning away from her conversation with Don.

"Nothing," Cory said, rummaging in his bag. He wasn't really looking for anything—he just didn't want to look up.

The game began and Cory turned his focus to Elizabeth, who was once again a starting forward for the high school team.

Everyone chatted for a while after the game, and then they all headed for the parking lot. "See you all first thing tomorrow?" Nancy said.

Tomorrow morning they were attending the local business networking meeting. It was the first time they would all attend together, and Cory was looking forward to it. The meetings were early in the morning, so he would only have to miss an hour or two of work. Things at the office were insane again, and Cory was nervous about being away for too long.

Milo and Rebecca were hosting this week's networking meeting at their café. It was quiet there in the early morning, and a little too chilly to sit out on the patio. The group was growing too large anyway. Cory arrived a little late, distracted, and wasn't able to sit near Nancy or the others. Instead, he sat at the end of the table and introduced himself to the gentleman next to him. They chatted and sipped coffee, waiting for the meeting to begin.

Milo and Rebecca had been attending this group for years. One guy in particular, they'd mentioned to Cory, was always asking for leads. However, he had never actually given anyone else a lead, according to Rebecca. It had become a bit of a inside joke in the group.

Sure enough, today Cory was next to that guy. And true to form, the man talked all about himself and his business, asking Cory if he knew anyone who could use his service. Ordinarily Cory would have gone out of his way to redirect him, but he just shook his head and went silent. The man turned to the person on the other side and carried on the conversation as if Cory wasn't even there.

Cory glanced longingly at his friends at the other end of the table. Finally, he left. "Got to get to work," he texted Nancy. "See you at the opportunity meeting tonight."

"That's strange," Nancy said to Rebecca. "Cory seems really disengaged lately. I hope everything is OK."

CHAPTER 13

Let Me Tell You a Story

When he arrived at the opportunity meeting that evening, Cory was surprised to see Nancy on stage, talking to Big Eye. They spotted Cory, and Big Eye waved as Nancy made her way down to Cory's seat.

"I'm going to speak next time!" Nancy said excitedly. "Big Eye wants me to talk about transitioning from corporate America to self-employment!"

Cory was genuinely happy for his friend, but deep down wondered why Big Eye hadn't asked him. But then, Cory hadn't exactly left corporate America, had he? He was still slogging to work every day in the city. Nancy had left her partnership at the law firm a few months ago. She had been an immediate success with the network marketing company, bringing in her friends, family, and clients to work with her. She was excited and deeply involved in the business, and her belief in the business model was off the charts.

Nancy was brimming with excitement as she greeted Milo and Rebecca with her news, and the four of them chatted while they waited for the meeting to begin.

As usual, Big Eye's approach to the microphone silenced the crowd.

"Let me tell you a story," he began. Laughter rippled through the crowd as everyone settled down to listen.

"When I worked on Wall Street, there was one broker who sat right next to me who started suddenly acting and speaking differently. He had much more conviction now than he'd had before when he closed trades, and he took charge when necessary. Within a short span of time, he seemed to transition from just 'one of the guys' to one of the leaders.

"One day we were casually discussing some news, and he brought up the subject of 'personal development.' He shared with me a program he'd recently completed. It was the Anthony Robbins 30-day cassette program from late-night TV. My first reaction echoed that of many at the time: 'C'mon—really? That giant rah-rah guy at 2 a.m.? Isn't he just another charlatan selling dreams?' But the more he told me about what he was learning and how it was helping him in his career, the more I was interested in listening to this program. I couldn't argue with the positive changes I'd seen in my co-worker.

"He stressed the importance of committing to the whole program, though, and said I could not miss even one day. The program included five one-hour tapes a week for four weeks in a row. No excuses. And I wouldn't really need one. Who wouldn't have time for one tape a day? He could easily give me a tape a day because I sat right next to him. He would let me have the next tape only if I'd listened to the previous night's tape, and I had no reason to lie. Who would I be kidding if I did that? And since we traded all day long on the Street together, we would never lie to each other anyway.

"Well, now that I think about it, for some reason it seemed okay to exaggerate the results of the weekend's golf game." Big Eye chuckled along with the crowd.

"Anyway, the 30 days flew by, and only a few times did I find it truly inconvenient to listen, but I budgeted my time and got it done. It opened up a fascinating and expansive new world for me. At the time, I didn't know anything about structured personal growth programs and didn't know it was a science. I had never even heard of the *Think and Grow Rich* guru Napoleon Hill, or countless other success stories out there. I guess I assumed that people such as Henry Ford and Thomas Edison were just smart and lucky. I didn't know they were also deep thinkers, constantly searching for what it takes to succeed.

"So the Robbins program was a huge turning point for me. It made me think in an entirely different way. I began to realize I had a lot more to learn about 'peak performance.' On Wall Street, I was surrounded by all types of talented people—some who had Ivy League educations, some who'd barely graduated from high school, and others in between. The ones who were thriving had figured out aspects of life they hadn't learned in college or on the streets. They had a handle on the 'mental game.' The tape program taught me that even ordinary people can achieve extraordinary things if they have a mental game plan.

"I remember thinking during those first 30 days of the tapes that probably a large percentage of the people who paid full price for the series never finished it. I was fully determined not to be among them. Heck, I got the tapes for free, and I still finished every single one. I guess the timing was right for me; I was ready to take my life up a notch.

"During that first month, I began each day even better than before. I was in a better mood and more thoughtful and respectful to family, friends, and strangers. I recall feeling like I was unstoppable—that not only could I achieve great things for myself and my family, but for others too. The program had given me grand ideas about life, and I had determined where I wanted to be in five and 10 years. Best of all, it opened my eyes to start working on my Plan B. I was newly married, and my wife and I planned on having a family soon. Did I want to keep working these super stressful 60- to 80-hour weeks? I had lots of grumpy colleagues in their mid and late 30s who weren't healthy or happy. Would that be me in 10 years? Besides, what good is having children if you can't spend quality time with them? My colleagues with children never saw them in the morning because they had to leave for work before 6 a.m. Often they wouldn't get home until 7:30 or 8 p.m., just as the toddlers were going to sleep.

"I knew a few people who took less stressful and lower-paying jobs within the trading field, but then their spouses had to work and they had to hire a nanny. My wife and I didn't want to settle for this. We both grew up with a mom at home and wanted our kids to have that luxury. The Robbins program allowed us to see that we could have it all.

"Of course, he's not the only one who trains in personal development. But the program led me to become an Anthony Robbins junkie, reading all his books and listening to his tapes over and over again. It's amazing to me how many people buy self-help books or business career books and never read more than a chapter or two. It's about following through. You might discover only one small technique in the book, but it could change your life. Becoming a Robbins fan also involved attending many of his seminars. And yes, I was at the live event where we learned to walk barefoot on hot coals without being burned. In fact, I have done it many times now and so have my wife and kids! Anyone here tonight who has done this program?"

Big Eye raised his hand, and about a dozen people in the audience raised their hands with him. Several people leaped up and cheered, waving wildly. It had clearly been an inspiring experience for them!

"Not only did I benefit from Tony himself, but through him, I gained another guide on my journey. At one of the first Robbins events I attended, I noticed my old friend Bob in the front row. I knew Bob from the local gym during my college days, and we reconnected. He had partnered with Robbins and had become Tony's most successful independent trainer and coach.

"I asked Bob how he'd gotten so involved with Robbins, and why. He told me he thought the best way to enhance his personal growth was to not only master the technology, but to teach it. When you do big things with great people, you will see big and great results. Surround yourself with these types of people and watch your life change for the better. This whole experience helped me to change my mindset. Like many of you, I was more than a little afraid of what other people might think of me if I introduced them to network marketing. I was afraid of being called a 'scammer,' or whatever label people would try to pin on me. But even this introduction to the world of personal development didn't sway me over to network marketing right away, believe it or not!"

Big Eye must have felt the audience was too quiet, so he asked a question he knew would get a rise out of them.

"Anyone here from New York?" he asked. Again, the crowd raised a cheer that lasted almost a minute.

Big Eye settled into a tall barstool in the middle of the stage as he continued his story.

"I was raised in a middle-class family in New York. My parents sacrificed a lot so I could go to good schools, a good college. From a very young age, my goal was to work on Wall Street as a trader. And I got there!" he said. "I used to trade hundreds of millions of dollars every few minutes in the foreign currency markets. Not right away, of course. I started out getting coffee, coming in early, staying late—I did whatever it took to get where I wanted to be. My bosses were making multiple six figures. Within two years I was a senior trader at the age of 23. I was making 10 times the money some of my college friends were. I thought it was the best job in the world! All my friends were either jealous or happy for me. I had plenty of spending money and routinely went out on the town on my brokers' expense accounts."

Man, he could be talking about me, Cory thought.

Big Eye continued. "I was living in New York City and

spending a lot of money on rent but it was a small fraction of what I was earning. I was proud of myself. My parents were proud. I thought I'd gotten lucky. A lot of my friends were smarter than me, working their way up as engineers or in pre-law, going to school at night, or going back for their MBA or law degree. Meanwhile, I was making major money. But every once in a while, there would be a huge setback. I'd get passed over for a position I wanted or realize my job was on the cutting block. I was even fired from one position. I had a real bad day on August 2, 1990, when Iraq invaded Kuwait. Happened to be short instead of long at that exact moment. I lost my entire year's profits in about five minutes and never really recovered mentally. Even though I was hugely successful from a young age, it seemed I was always one bad decision away from getting the axe. Talk about stress."

Milo leaned over to Cory. "This guy really does understand your world! I can't even imagine playing with those stakes," he said, admiration clear in his voice.

"After 10 years of living this 'dream life,' my wife and I started having children. I realized this lifestyle was not for me. I had to spend three hours in the car every day—an hour and a half each way. And that was before cell phones! I missed my kids. In the morning I left for work before they woke up, and I'd stop at the gym on my way home. So I didn't get home until 6:30 or 7 on a good night, and often after 8, when they'd already gone to bed. I started to notice some of the guys at work, who weren't that much older than me, starting to look way older than they were. Stress!

"But still, why would I quit? I had no idea about fulfillment, about helping and mentoring people. Once in a while I'd mentor a kid who was getting coffee, teach him some tricks of the trade. But I wasn't serving thousands of people. I wasn't serving anyone, actually, although my mission was commendable by anyone's measure. I was trying to make a good living for my family. We had a good home, I was saving money to pay for college and vacations, and, hopefully, enough to retire a little early. That was my goal. I was just buying low and selling high, and pulling my hair out. It was just digits on the screen, trying to make money for my bank so the bank could give me a bigger bonus so I could save it and retire earlier than most people. That's it."

Cory was nodding almost continuously as Big Eye talked. This really was his life!

"When I discovered network marketing, and really dove into the model, it turned my world upside down. You're actually helping people become more financially secure, and to get out of their comfort zones. Not just one or two people, like on the trading desk, but thousands—your reach could be tens of thousands of people. A lot has changed in this decade, where you can now run a multi-million dollar business from your smartphone."

Big Eye stood and slipped a slim phone out of his pocket and held it up. "Anyone else use this office?" Again, cheers and clapping erupted.

"I used to regret waiting so long to get into network marketing," Big Eye said. "What was I afraid of? Why are so many people afraid? One of the greatest phrases our founding fathers used more than 200 years ago was, 'The pursuit of happiness.'

Aren't we all entitled to be happy? Or at least to pursue happiness? I think that's the problem: People think they are 'entitled' to be happy, but most people do not *pursue* it. Or they think they are pursuing happiness by studying hard and trying to get a good job and play the 'employment' game. But this rarely leads to true fulfillment and happiness."

I sure don't see a lot of happy people at work, Cory thought. *Maybe that's why they keep saying they work hard "for their family."*

"My industry was changing rapidly and I could see that technology would soon make our jobs obsolete. There used to be hundreds of banks trading, and now we were down to three to four dozen. By age 30, I was part of the management team, deciding who would be let go each month. It was becoming harder to make money as a trader. My final year on Wall Street, I worked twice as hard and made less money. Right then, I realized I would have to do something else. I'm not wired to be in an industry where I can't make more money every year. I believe if I get better, I deserve to attract more income. Sometimes you're stuck in the wrong vehicle—in the wrong job, wrong profession, and you become obsolete. You need to be three years ahead. Well, I found out I was three years behind. I wish I'd found network marketing then, but I didn't.

"I went into a traditional business ownership, took a loan against my house, and started a payroll and benefits company. I went a full year without pay, traded my deluxe Lexus for a lime green Corolla, and worried constantly about paying the mortgage. I knew this was good for me and I was learning a lot, but man, was it stressful!

"Network marketing was in my line of sight, but the truth is, I wasn't ready. I'm not sure if I could have survived network marketing before technology brought us cell phones and the Internet. But I always kept an open mind on the business. There were billion dollar companies that had multi-million dollar earners and I respected them; it just wasn't for me.

"By the time I realized what a great profession network marketing is, I just didn't really care what people thought. I had gone to college; I put in my time and got the degree. But there are still people who know I make six figures a month—per month, not per year—and they still look at me like I'm nuts.

> But there are still people who know I make six figures a month—per month, not per year—and they still look at me like I'm nuts.

I don't believe they understand the network marketing model. If this is the reality for any of you, you're going to have to get over that. What are you afraid of? No one is going to shoot you. You're just going to get a couple of no's and a couple of confused people. That's their problem. Not yours. So if you really want to get serious, we'll just have to dig deeper. You'll just have to have an open mind and an open heart, because this could be a very important day in your life."

Big Eye replaced the microphone in the stand, but then turned back to the crowd.

"I'm glad you're all here. Let's keep digging in. If you're happy and comfortable, you're never going to grow. I want to see if I can get you very uncomfortable, that you take the plunge and go into a territory that you've never gone into before. Because that's what I did. I can tell you, it's terrifying. But once you get to the other side, it's wonderful. It never stops. You're constantly growing, pushing yourself, giving speeches, making videos, writing books, coming up with ways to help people. There is a better way to live and work. Do you have what it takes?"

Big Eye raised his hand in a salute to the crowd as the roar of applause overtook the room. He then introduced a guest speaker, a relative newcomer to the business who was building a huge business.

Cory glanced at his watch and whispered to Nancy, "I need to get going. Big client meeting in the morning. See you guys later." With a little wave to Milo and Rebecca, Cory left.

CHAPTER 14

Doubt Takes Over

At his morning meeting, Cory was surprised to see Bill walk in at the last minute. He quickly looked down at his notebook so he wouldn't have to greet his tormentor. What the hell? he thought. This is my meeting! Cory looked up and gazed levelly at Bill, who smirked in return. I am not going to let Bill get to me, Cory thought with firm resolve. He rose confidently, and started the meeting.

Things had gotten progressively busier at work, and the hostility from Bill and the others had escalated seriously since the retreat. There was another retreat coming up, and Cory was really dreading it. As a manager, though, not only was Cory attending, he was a presenter this year. It made him sick to his stomach to think about it.

Cory ended the meeting and quickly shut himself in his office, working furiously to catch up. But he just couldn't stop thinking about Bill and the others. Their hostility was puzzling to him. They had been really good friends just a year ago! Cory left his desk and started walking to the corner hot dog stand—he had to get Bill and the other immature jerks off his mind.

"Hey Cory!" He paled as he realized Bill and his friends were walking just a few steps behind him.

"How's the delusional business these days?" Bill asked. "I'm surprised you can eke out any time out for your 'real' job."

"Yeah, how goes the scamming? Gonna get some Kool-Aid with your dog today?" asked Taylor. "Talk any little old ladies out of any fortunes lately?" The guys laughed. Cory stopped abruptly, and turned to face them.

"Come on, guys," Cory said. "It was just a little side trip into another business. I'm not even that active in it anymore. Like I have any extra time after being here all day and half the night." They started walking again, but Cory turned at the corner, deciding to bypass lunch for now. "See you guys at the retreat," he said, walking quickly in the opposite direction.

Was that what he was doing? Cory wondered. Was he taking advantage of people? Drinking the Kool-Aid, as the saying goes? Maybe it was a scam. But look at Big Eye. That guy was for real. And Dave. Semi-retired! Nancy was doing really well, and she was a lawyer. She'd know if this was illegal or shady. But really, the guys have a point: Think of all the years I spent in school. I worked so hard for that degree! Am I wasting my time?

Cory reached his building and punched the elevator button. Maybe the guys were right. Maybe if he just buckled down and really focused on this Wall Street job, he could land in a different department where he would be appreciated.

On the way up to his office, Cory's phone beeped. An email from Nancy: "Hey Cory, the back office appears to be down.

Have you heard anything from the company? Or have you tried getting into your website? Let me know!"

Great. Now the company website was his problem too? There were just too many problems. The elevator doors opened at his floor. Cory ignored the email and got back to work, this time preparing his presentation for the retreat, which was quickly approaching.

A few days later, Cory settled himself into his seat on the commuter plane taking everyone upstate to the retreat. Even though the guys had eased up a bit since their run-in on the street, Cory was anxious to get his presentation over with and get on with the pressing business of Wall Street. He had gotten a promotion, had a new team in a new department, and a new enthusiasm for his work. Cory actually looked forward to going to work, and even to his commute now, which gave him at least a one-hour stretch of uninterrupted time where he could focus on improving his mind. He had to give Big Eye credit for that. Cory never left for work without a fresh audiobook—some were on CDs that Big Eye had loaned him, and some Cory had downloaded directly onto his phone.

Big Eye was also generous in loaning out his favorite inspirational paperback books, only asking that people return them to him when they were done, or pass them along to a sincerely interested prospect. Cory had quite a few of these in his library as well. He made a mental note to send Big Eye a text and set up a time to return the books.

As the plane took off, Cory started thinking about Nancy and his other friends from soccer and the neighborhood. He felt a little guilty for stepping away so abruptly, but also, they had to understand: He was just using his education, his training. He had tried network marketing though, and made it through some rough patches, especially sticking with it even after the first retreat. He should get credit for that, shouldn't he? Really, the last straw had been his father-in-law saying, "What, you're just throwing away all that education? All those years on the Street? For a little home-based business? Cory. C'mon." And then dismissing Cory with a disgusted wave.

Cory had tried to present his point in a different way, but his father-in-law just held up his hand and said, scornfully, "Cory, I will *never* do network marketing."

Network marketing just wasn't for me, Cory told himself. And really, I just can't do everything.

The plane started its descent and he started to mentally prepare to head for the lodge that had created such a nightmare just a few months ago. As the plane taxied in, he got out his phone and sent a quick text to Big Eye, asking about a good time to return the books.

"Hey Cory," a familiar voice greeted him as he walked into the lodge. Cory tensed as a few of the guys from the last retreat approached.

"Hey, man, we just want to apologize for coming down on you so hard last time," Bill said. "It was just a shock that someone as educated as you are would put any credence into a home-based business."

"Yeah," added Taylor, throwing an arm around Cory's shoulder as they all walked toward the reception area. "But dude, seriously, we want to talk to you. What are you doing? You're throwing away your talent. Wasting your education. Ruining your life. You've worked really hard to get where you are."

"You have a new department now," Bill added. "It wouldn't be good for the guys at the top to find out you were involved in a part-time sales thing, even if it was 100 percent legit."

The others nodded, and Cory sipped his drink. They were probably right. And besides, he had heard nothing but problems from all of his friends and downline who had joined. The website's down. There's a problem with the product. Was that all his responsibility too?

Aloud, Cory replied, "Yeah, I've really been rethinking all of that. I'm glad you guys didn't get sucked in. I've stepped away and I'm just concentrating on my new job."

Taylor slapped him on the back and they all raised their glasses in a toast.

"Here's to regaining your sanity," Bill said. They all laughed, and then turned their attention to a passing tray of hors d'oeuvres.

This is probably for the best, Cory thought. *I've made my money back and honestly, I'm tired of working so hard, day and night. Let Nancy carry it on. She's the one on stage now, after all.*

CHAPTER 15

An Entrepreneur Who Happens to Be a Lawyer

Nancy was on fire. She was speaking regularly at events with Big Eye now, and her team was growing exponentially. Milo and Rebecca were not far behind, and often joined her on stage to talk about their unlikely foray into network marketing. All three were now making full-time income working part-time. From time to time they reached out to Cory, but never got a response. He hadn't been spotted at a soccer game all season, and they hadn't seen him at the restaurant or in town either.

This evening, Big Eye was again slated to speak to the group, and Nancy was scheduled to go on right after him. Nancy's husband Jeff had come with her tonight; he wanted to see this Big Eye guy for himself, and, of course, to lend his support to Nancy.

Big Eye's phone beeped, and a text from Cory came in: "Hey Big Eye, I just realized I still have a bunch of books you loaned me, and I'm going to be really tied up with work for the foreseeable future. Is there a good time to return them to you?" Big Eye had noticed Cory's absence from the business and events, but encouraged the others to power on through Cory's ambivalence. He shook his head and switched off his phone, getting ready to go on stage.

Nancy and the others had indeed powered through, and their businesses had exploded. Several of Nancy's law clients who had joined her in the business were nearby in the audience. She smiled and waved at a group sitting slightly behind them, and received a thumbs-up in return. "I can't believe I was worried that they would think I'd be less committed as their lawyer," she said to Rebecca.

"Did all of your clients join you?" Rebecca asked.

"Not everyone, although I did approach all of my clients," Nancy said. "But those who didn't want to move forward with the business seem a little closer now. I think they see me as an entrepreneur now, and not just their lawyer. I just told them I'm approached with business opportunities every so often and I always take a look, but that this one really interested me. And I always asked for their opinion, as astute businesspeople. Some loved it and some only liked it and said the timing just wasn't right. A couple seemed to be neutral. But none of them told me I was crazy! And no one dropped me as their attorney."

> She is really an entrepreneur who also happens to be a lawyer.

"Honestly, I was worried about that," Jeff piped up. "When Nancy told me she was going to talk to her law clients, I was afraid she would ruin her reputation as a lawyer. But then she explained that she is really an entrepreneur who also happens to be a lawyer, and that's how she presented it to her clients. I was happy to be wrong, for once!" Jeff slipped his arm around Nancy's shoulder, giving her a light squeeze.

Milo leaned over Rebecca to ask, "Where the heck is Cory?" Nancy shook her head and said, "He's at a another company retreat. He probably didn't want to miss this, but he is giving a presentation at the retreat." In truth, Cory had been MIA for a long time. He wasn't answering emails or calls, either.

Today Big Eye was speaking about self-talk, belief, and giving. The title of his speech was, "Change your language, and you'll change your direction."

He began by encouraging everyone to think about the language they use, all the time. "Think about this," Big Eye said. "How often do you say to yourself, 'I've *got* to—(fill in the blank).' Try this instead: 'I *get* to (fill in the blank).' Here's an example. Try simply saying, 'I *get* to go to the gym four times a week,' instead of, 'I've *got* to go to the gym four times a week.' Heck, some people don't have the time or the money to join a gym. Maybe they have a disability and can't even work out. So instead of saying, 'I've *got* to take my mom shopping on Saturday morning,' you can say, 'I *get* to take my mom shopping.' Some people who have lost their mothers would give a lot to *get* to take their mom shopping. You see how one word—in this case just one letter, changing the word '*got*' to '*get*'—can have such a powerful influence on your mood? The words we use are so important. A lot of people say knowledge is power. But I believe action is power. There's a lot of knowledge out there. Libraries are filled with books. The Internet is filled with crazy amounts of information. The banks are filled with money. But if you don't take action and find ways to connect the dots, all the knowledge in the world doesn't matter. Change your language and your life will change in powerful ways. In network marketing we're always looking for go-getters. But soon you want to get people who are go-getters and turn them into go-givers."

Nancy, Milo, and Rebecca quickly wrote that line in their notebooks.

"Network marketing works best when you go from a student to a mentor as fast as you can," Big Eye said. "Become a student of the game as fast as you can, and then become a mentor. But you will find that being a student also never ends. In this profession you will always be learning, giving, and mentoring."

> In network marketing we're always looking for go-getters. But soon you want to get people who are go-getters and turn them into go-givers.

Big Eye finished his short speech to wild applause, as usual, and then invited Nancy to the stage.

"Tonight I want to talk about getting what you deserve," she began, emphasizing the word deserve. Nancy was a natural leader, and now was blossoming into a great speaker; the audience stilled at her powerful introductory line. "The word 'de-serve' actually means 'from serving.' A lot of people have funny connotations surrounding money. People think they don't deserve money. They'll ask, 'Do I really deserve a nice car and vacation spot when there are so many people suffering in the world?' The answer is yes: If you've earned it, you deserve it. As we learn and grow in this profession, we see people like Big Eye, who participate all the time in humanitarian missions. Does he serve? Every day. I will always be grateful to him for introducing the person who in turn introduced me to the business. This business has allowed me to leave the corporate world and be at home full-time. I work around my children's schedules, and give back whenever I can. It's helped me be a better mother and citizen. You have to believe that you can create this life for yourself."

Beaming, Jeff walked over to the stairs to offer a hand as Nancy stepped down from the stage to a thunderous standing ovation. Big Eye hugged her as Nancy and Jeff returned to their seats in the front row, next to Milo and Rebecca.

CHAPTER 16

Energy Infusion

Thousands of animated people were filing into the convention hall for the company's annual convention. Backstage, Nancy and Big Eye could hear and feel the pulse of high-energy music pumping enthusiasm into the already highly excited crowd. Nancy had the honor of introducing Big Eye for his keynote address.

"I wish Cory was here," Nancy said suddenly. "I owe all of this to him."

"Nancy, believe it or not, this happens all the time," Big Eye said. "And you've worked really hard to get where you are! People get started in the business and then they cave in to peer pressure, or family pressure, or work pressure—whatever got to Cory is heartbreaking, but it happens all the time. He brought you into the business, right?"

Nancy smiled. "That's true. I just feel bad that he quit right before everything took off," she said.

The convention producer stuck her head into the green room. "Five-minute warning!" she said brightly. "Ready?"

Nancy gave an excited thumbs-up, and with a quick hug from Big Eye, walked over to the entrance at stage left where they had rehearsed just a day before. At the signal, Nancy strode confidently to center stage, and flawlessly introduced Big Eye. He joined her onstage as the convention production company cranked up the volume on his favorite song. He gave a thumbs-up to the stage crew and hugged Nancy.

As Nancy left the stage, Big Eye delivered his trademark line.

"Let me tell you a story," Big Eye began, and the audience roared. "Actually, today I want to talk about leaving a legacy. When I say legacy, you probably think about famous names—Carnegie, Rockefeller and Ford—or maybe a tradition, your mom's gravy, your dad's work ethic. But let's talk about real legacy. Remember my cousin Vito? You've all heard that story, right?"

Again, the audience cheered wildly.

"Talk about leaving a legacy! Not only did he accomplish his dream, he brought his extended family along with him. Then, he continued to build and help his sleepy hometown become a booming, vital city. Do you think he left a legacy? I'll bet his townspeople think so! There are a lot of ways to leave a legacy. We're not just talking about famous people who leave huge sums of money to good causes, and who get museums and hospitals named after them. You can leave a legacy with an antique car you've been working on for years. Or with a family recipe, handed down for generations and perfected by you. We're not talking about money that you leave for your children or relatives.

"But let's talk about real legacy—the impression you leave on people for the rest of their life. What's great about network marketing—what's so powerful about it—is that you create your own legacy in this business, good or bad. In this business, you'll always get those people who think this is a get-rich-quick deal. They're in and out of deals quickly, and drag people in who maybe can't afford what they're offering right now. This hurts people, and really hurts the reputation of the profession. Those folks leave a really bad legacy, in all ways," Big Eye said.

He paused for dramatic effect and to let the murmuring in the audience die down.

"But let's focus on the positive part of network marketing and the legacy you can leave," Big Eye continued. "When you sign up people who are better than you and grow faster than you, they are grateful to you. If it wasn't for you showing them this business at the time you did, they may not have been successful. They are very grateful to you!"

Big Eye had walked to center stage, and looked pointedly for a moment at Nancy, Milo, and Rebecca in the front row. Nancy realized he had changed his speech for her!

Stepping back to the center of the stage again, Big Eye continued. "I know because it happened to me. Of the people who showed me the business, some are very successful and some aren't. But I am grateful to all of them. I am a self-made millionaire. The money's great! But for me, it's really about who I became in the process of making that money. It wasn't by mistake. Those who get lucky, like the people who win the lottery, tend to lose it or blow it. They don't treasure it.

"This business is about the person you become. In making my money, I have learned the power of improving myself every day. Personal development is the most important part of my day, and I never stop learning. The more you do for yourself, learn for yourself, the more people you can serve. And the more you do for others, the more you get in return. I truly believe that. When you freely give, you freely receive.

"You thinking about getting rich? It doesn't work that way. Think about becoming a bigger and better person and everything you want will flow. The good health, the money, relationships—it all flows effortlessly.

"If you really want to make your network marketing business explode, become a student, become a mentor, teach other people to become mentors, and then create a team of people who think like we think. But just like Vito, when you've reached your goal, you need to say, 'What next? Who can I help? What am I going to do to take massive action today?' The people you know deserve it, and you certainly deserve it as well.

"Remember my story about how I was introduced to network marketing? How I rolled my eyes, and told my mentor, 'I will *never* do network marketing?' Well here I am!" He held his arms out in an expansive gesture to the crowd.

Big Eye had to wait nearly two minutes for the cheers to die down so he could continue.

"Well, for 20 years I'd roll my eyes at anyone who mentioned network marketing and I'd say, 'That is not for me. I will *never* do network marketing!' Finally I saw the light, and look where I am today. I want to help guys like me, who have negative connotations of network marketing. I want them to see that I ended up making six figures a month in the first year! Now granted, that's highly unusual. It takes most people a lot longer than that. I just happened to have a great business partner, a wife and family who believed intensely in me, and a drive to dig in and make this opportunity work. When I finally saw the light, technology had made network marketing so much easier in so many ways. And I was beyond frustrated with the day-to-day, around-the-clock hassle of running a traditional brick-and-mortar business. And, I was done driving the lime green Corolla," he joked.

Big Eye knew most everyone in the audience had heard that story, and he paused for a sip of water as the crowd settled back down.

"A lot of people think this profession is for people who can't hold down a regular job. So what? Don't be afraid to show this model to mainstream people, and don't worry when people make fun of you and tell you you're nuts. Some of them may come around and do network marketing. Just because one person rolls their eyes at the mention of a business opportunity, don't give up on it. I was that guy! Eventually they will see the light. There are people in every walk of life who are going to figure out that this is a legitimate profession."

> Just because one person rolls their eyes at the mention of a business opportunity, don't give up on it. I was that guy!

Big Eye raised his arms again as the music picked up and the emcee came out to introduce the next segment.

Nancy turned to Milo. "I still wish Cory was here!" she said.

"Me too, but I'm glad we are all still here," Rebecca said.

CHAPTER 17

Leaving the Light On

Cory was late getting to the high school championship game. He walked slowly to the field, avoiding the area where he knew Nancy, Milo, and Rebecca would be sitting together. He was tired of all the questions. Frankly, he was just tired. Cory scanned the sidelines for Michelle and Michael, and spotted them, thankfully sitting toward the far end of the team's spectator section. Even though the late afternoon sun was dimming rapidly, Cory left his sunglasses on as he made his way over to sit by his wife and son. Even so, Nancy caught his eye and waved. She put her hands up in a, "Hey, what's up," gesture, and Cory just shrugged and waved. He took off his sunglasses and turned his attention to the game.

Elizabeth's team won the game, but it was way closer than had been predicted. Suddenly, Nancy appeared at Cory's elbow.

"Hey stranger!" she said brightly. "Hi Michelle, Michael! I hope you guys will come over. We're having a little party after the game. Please join us."

Michelle agreed quickly, before Cory could say anything.

Cory was afraid he'd be cornered and asked to explain himself, but Milo and Rebecca just hugged him and quickly congratulated the girls.

"We've got to get over to the café," they explained. "We've got an employee appreciation party going on right now. Good to see you Cory! You too Michelle." Nancy offered to drive their daughter home, and they were off, hand in hand, as the others left for the victory party.

At the house, Nancy again welcomed Cory and Michelle warmly, and then returned to her guests. Realizing there would be no inquisition, Cory relaxed, and started to enjoy the evening, watching Elizabeth celebrate the win with her teammates. As they were getting ready to leave, Michelle went to find Michael, who was out in the yard kicking around a soccer ball with the championship team. Cory picked up the cups littered around the family room, and carried them to the kitchen where Nancy was rinsing some plates.

"Cory, I am so grateful to you!" Nancy said. "And not just for bringing in the cups!" They both laughed as Cory handed Nancy the dirty cups. "This year has been an absolute blessing, and I wouldn't even have known about this wonderful opportunity if you hadn't been brave enough to introduce it to me. I've been wanting to tell you that for a while, but you've been—well, you've just been so busy."

Cory didn't know what to say.

"It's OK, Cory," Nancy said. "Big Eye understands too. He's told me he's been where you are, and it's tough. You need to do what you feel is right. But truly, Cory, thank you from the bottom of my heart."

"Of course, Nancy," Cory finally said. She gave him a quick hug and went out into the yard to say goodbye to Michelle.

Just then Cory's phone chimed with a new text message, from Big Eye. It had been a while since Cory had sent the text about returning the books and he hadn't had a response. Cory had figured Big Eye was just really disappointed in him.

"Hey Cory," Big Eye wrote. "Your text came in while I was onstage a while back and I just kept forgetting to text you back! Hope you're well. Bring the books anytime. You know where I live. If I'm not there or it's late, just leave them on the porch. My porch light is always on."

As they arrived home, the kids hopped out of the car and ran ahead into the house.

"I'm just going to return some books I borrowed from Big Eye," Cory said. "I've been meaning to for a long time. You mind if I just go now, while I'm thinking of it?"

"No, of course not. It's late though," Michelle said. "Will he be there?"

"He said to come by anytime; he'll leave a light on for me," Cory said.

Cory backed the car out of the driveway and started over to Big Eye's home, which was just a few miles away. He'd been putting off returning the books, worried about having to have a difficult conversation and explain his departure from the company.

But Nancy's kind welcome tonight had made him realize that she was truly grateful to Cory, and their friendship was intact. And Big Eye wasn't upset after all.

As he drove, Cory reflected on the past year. He was sure he'd made the right decision. Hadn't he? He had to focus on his job.

You did make the right decision, yes, of course you did, Cory told himself.

The trip took longer than he expected, and it was really late as he pulled into Big Eye's driveway. There were no lights on inside the house, but true to his word, the porch light was on.

Cory had wrapped the books in a plastic bag in case he would have to leave them outside, and as he leaned down to set the package on the small table by the door, he saw a note. It was addressed to him.

He read, "Thanks for returning the books, Cory. I hope you enjoyed them as much as I loved sharing them with you. The porch light will always be on for you. All the best, Big Eye."

About the Author

Joe Occhiogrosso is one of the most successful network marketing professionals in the world today. A converted life-long "pyramid scam" skeptic from New York City, he is one of the few people in network marketing history to build a seven-figure residual income in less than one year.

Joe graduated from Rutgers University with degrees in Economics and Philosophy, and the "Mr. Rutgers" bodybuilding title, at the age of 20. He immediately engaged on a ten-year wild ride on Wall Street trading in the 24-hour global currency markets for major banks.

After the birth of his first child, he started tiring of the one-hour-plus commute, along with the stress of the 24-hour currency trading markets, and decided to start his own traditional business in the suburbs. Joe spent the next five years building a successful payroll and benefits company. He was bought out by a group of private investors, and then started a title insurance agency and grew it to one of the best in his home state.

Along the way he had been approached with dozens of network marketing opportunities, but he never really gave the profession much serious thought. Then finally, in 2009 he decided that network marketing was indeed a better way. He decided to go all in, and really become a student of the game.

Now Joe has come full circle and spends most of his time training and coaching traditional business leaders on how to become network marketing professionals.

For Joe, success begins and ends with others.

"At the end of the day, it's not about rising above others or leaving them in your wake; it's about how many people you bring along with you," Joe said. "Ride your vision, give before you get, invest in yourself and others, and learn how to network."

Joe lives in northern New Jersey with his wife Annmarie, and their three children. Joe enjoys spending time with his family, playing baseball, and serving on the fundraising committee for St. Jude's Children's Hospital. He also participates in his company's annual mission trips to underdeveloped countries.

Connect with Joe:
www.joeobook.com
Facebook.com/joeobook
twitter.com/joeocchio
email: joeobook@gmail.com